Adult-

ery

and Other Diversions

Adult-ery

and Other Diversions

Tim Parks

Arcade Publishing • New York

This edition first published in the United Kingdom in 1998 by Secker & Warburg

"Adultery" first appeared in *The New Yorker*, June 24, 1996
"Fidelity" first appeared in *The New Yorker*, December 23, 1996
"Analogies" first appeared in *The New Yorker*, April 27, 1998

Arcade Publishing books may be purchased in bulk at special discounts for sales promotion, corporate gifts, fund-raising, or educational purposes. Special editions can also be created to specifications. For details, contact the Special Sales Department, Arcade Publishing, 307 West 36th Street, 11th Floor, New York, NY 10018 or arcade@skyhorsepublishing.com.

Arcade Publishing® is a registered trademark of Skyhorse Publishing, Inc.®, a Delaware corporation.

Visit our website at www.arcadepub.com.

10 9 8 7 6 5 4 3 2 1

Library of Congress Cataloging-in-Publication Data is available on file.

ISBN: 978-1-61145-821-3

Printed in the United States of America

Contents

Author's Note

In the course of some desultory reading over the last year or so, and that is since completing the pieces that make up this collection, I think I can safely say that I have come across every idea here expressed, and more often than not in the writings of two centuries, or even two millennia ago. So the reader can rest assured that he will not have to tackle anything new in these pages. But novelty is an ambition one long since learned to set aside. No, my hope when I began work on these odd hybrids was rather to dramatize an intimate relation between reflections that are timeless and the ongoing stories of our lives. Schopenhauer was not alone in remarking that rather than developing concepts in response to direct experience, we are taught them abstractly in youth so that there is often 'little correspondence between our ideas, which have been fixed by mere words, and the real knowledge we have acquired through perception'. For most of us many years must pass before those two areas of consciousness can be anything more than casual acquaintances, our greatest illuminations often coming when finally we have the experience — a love, a death, a moment with our children — that fits the concept, or at last the concept is seen from the angle that matches our experience. It is then, with a sense of exhilaration and sometimes horror, that we come into full possession of what we now discover we only thought we knew. In their attempt to evade the distinction between narrative and essay, or to have the one form call constantly to the other, these pieces grope towards such illuminations.

Adultery

A couple of years ago I found myself listening to a lecture on the somewhat abstruse theme: 'Marriage Bedroom Tapestries in the Works of Shakespeare: *Othello*, *The Winter's Tale*, *Cymbeline*'. It's not the kind of thing I would generally move heaven and earth to get to, but I was stuck in a conference centre outside Milan, it was raining heavily, there was nothing else to do. As it turned out, I was spellbound. With extraordinary vivacity, the speaker, a fine-looking woman in her fifties, used slides and video clips to illustrate the profound ambiguities of a series of images woven onto the upholstered bedsteads of the Elizabethan aristocracy. Particularly fascinating was the collision of sacred and profane, the scenes of domestic bliss undermined by evident allusions to more disturbing emotions: serpents and harpies warning rapturous newly-weds of obscure calamities to come. Then the speaker began to explain how Shakespeare had drawn on this material in his plays, but what she really ended up giving us was a whole history of marriage, from its dynastic origins when the family was everything and sentiments relegated to extramarital adventures, to the crisis sparked off by the tradition of courtly love when husbands and wives began to leave their partners to follow their lovers, and finally the search for a solution in the novel idea that marriage be founded on love rather than family. This last adventure, the speaker claimed, was the subject of the three plays she had selected for consideration, this the underlying theme of the allegories featured in the bedroom tapestries: the huge gamble of placing love at the heart of marriage, the sad discovery, fearfully embodied in *Othello*, that love is even more fragile than dynasty. All it took was an unexplained handkerchief, a jealous tempera-ment, and, as Shakespeare so timelessly put it, 'Farewell the tranquil mind, farewell content . . .'

After the lecture, chatting to two elderly professors, I couldn't help but praise the marvellous dispatch of the woman's delivery, the energy and passion and relevance of her analysis of marriage. 'A brilliant lecture,' I insisted. 'No mystery about that,' remarked one of the two. His smile was at once sad and wry. 'Her husband just left her for a twenty-two-year-old.'

Love and dynasty, passion and family. It was around this time that Alistair's story got into full swing. I was his confidant. We played squash together twice a week, then over beers afterwards he told me all about it. We were best friends. As he spoke, he was full of laughter and his face burned with excitement. 'You've blown your marriage,' I warned him. He laughed out loud and used sports terminol-ogy. Playing away. Scoring in extra time. Next week's game plan. The logistics can be so complicated, he chuckled. He even giggled. And you could see what an enormous sense of release he must have felt in this first affair after eight or nine years of marriage. Alistair was a very sober, a very solid, a very reliable man, but now the great dam of vows and virtue, the conventional vision of life he had grown up with, was crumbling beneath a tidal wave of Dionysiac excitement.

We worked together at the university and in the corridor I remember showing him a passage from a book I was translating, Calasso's *The Marriage of Cadmus and Harmony:* 'Dionysus,' it said, 'is not a useful god who helps weave or knot things together, but a god who loosens and unties. The weavers are his enemies. Yet there comes a moment when the weavers will abandon their looms to dash off after him into the mountains. Dionysus is the river we hear flowing by in the distance, an incessant booming from far away; then one day it rises and floods everything, as if the normal above-water state of things, the sober delimitation of our existence, were but a brief parenthesis overwhelmed in an instant.'

'You're possessed,' I told him. Alistair nodded and laughed. He had been a weaver for so long. He had woven together family-house-career-car. But the following evening, after squash again, he was describing how in that family car his girlfriend (though he always called her his 'mistress' – he liked that word) had pulled up her skirt – they were on the *autostrada* between Bergamo and Brescia – and started masturbating, then rubbed her scented hand across his face, pushed her fingers in his mouth. Since we live in Italy, and have both lived here a long time, he occasionally broke into Italian. '*Evviva le puttanelle!*' he laughed. 'Long live the little whores!' He was in love with

3

her. For those of us looking on, those of us still safely within wedlock's everyday limits, it's hard not to feel a mixture of trepidation and envy on seeing a friend in this state. Clearly it is very exciting when you start destroying everything.

Alistair referred to his wife as 'The Queen of Unreason' or 'She Who Must Be Obeyed'. His wife was still a weaver. They had two young children. With the way feminism has changed everything and nothing, it was she who was in charge at home, she who felt primarily responsible for the children. Men of course now help in the home and, being a reasonable and generous man, Alistair helped a great deal. But he was not in charge. Her conscientiousness and maternal anxiety, heightened no doubt by her decision to stay at work despite the kids, must frequently have looked like bossiness to him. Their arguments were entirely trivial: whose turn it was to do this or that. He felt himself the butt of her imperatives, his behaviour constantly under observation. It's difficult to make love in these circumstances. Or perhaps it was simply that with everything now achieved it was time for something else to happen. All of us have so much potential that will never be realized within the confines necessary to weave anything together. Job and marriage are our two greatest prisons. When he asked her what was wrong, how could he understand if she didn't tell, she said if only he spared her a moment's attention he would understand without being told. Every intimacy is a potential hell. Alistair referred to sex with his wife as 'duty-fucking'.

The affair began. Chiara was a young widow, thirty-three,

with a ten-year-old girl and an excellent job in education administration that took her to the same conferences Alistair attended. Rather than a decision, it was a question of opportunity coinciding with impulse, no, with a day when he felt he *deserved* this escape. Sex was new again. They made love in Rome, Naples, Geneva, Marseilles. They made love in cars, trains, boats. They made love in every possible way. No erotic stone was left unturned. Anal sex, water sports, mutual masturbation, I had to listen to it all. Then all the complicated logistics of their encounters, which seemed to be at least half the thrill. Advantages and disadvantages of mobile phones, the dangers of credit cards. They adored each other's bodies, inside and out. Alistair was in love with Chiara. She was so intelligent. Her black hair too! Wasn't she beautiful? Between love-making they had such intelligent conversations: philosophy, psychology, politics, their lives. They gave books to each other. They swapped stories. They experienced the delirium of all that information flowing back and forth, your own life retold, another life discovered. There is always something to talk about when one is falling in love. As so often there is not in the long-haul mechanics of marriage.

But how could Alistair leave his children? He loved his children, though his wife was becoming more and more difficult. Every now and then he would interrupt his long descriptions of carefully timed meetings and frantic sex with some self-justifying story of his wife's unreasonableness. Why did she always object to the way he did even the most trivial things, the way he hung a picture, the way he left his toothbrush – get this – turned outward from the toothglass, so it dripped on the floor, instead of inward so it didn't? Can you imagine! he protested. Not to mention the fact that she never gave him blowjobs. But Alistair admitted that he couldn't be sure any more whether his arguments with his wife were purely between themselves, or had to do with his mistress in some way. Perhaps he was deliberately stirring up these petty conflicts in order to justify his eventual departure. Perhaps they weren't arguing about a toothbrush at all. Things were getting mixed up. Out of nostalgia, or guilt, or perhaps just to see what it felt like, Alistair would try to be romantic with his wife. He would bring flowers. When the children were safely asleep he would persuade her to make love. And immediately he realized he didn't really want to make love to her. He felt no vigour, no zest. He wanted to be with his mistress. 'I told her I'd heard the baby coughing,' he laughed. But sadly.

Passion, family. Was it time for Alistair to leave home? I thought yes. He said when he and his wife sat together of an evening playing with the children or catching a movie on TV they were perfectly happy. Not to mention all the economic considerations. And perhaps the thing he had with Chiara couldn't be turned into long-term cohabitation. He lived in the frenzy of the choice unmade, the divided mind. Convinced he was trying to come to a decision, he relentlessly applied the kind of logic that was so effective in his research, as if this were a technical problem that could simply be solved. It's the kind of Cartesian inheritance that has filled the bookstores with self-help manuals: life a problem to solve if only you knew how. I was equally glib. 'You've just got to work out which means most to you,' I told him. 'Perhaps it's only sex with Chiara.' 'You must never put the word "only" in front of "sex",' he objected. 'Or not the kind we have. It's an absolute.' 'So, you're only staying at home for the children,' I tried. 'You should leave.' But now he said that you couldn't put the word 'only' in front of 'children' either. Passion and children were both absolutes. You couldn't weigh them against each other. In the end, Alistair managed to prolong a state of doubt and potential, of anything-can-happen precariousness, for nigh on eighteen months. Later he would appreciate it had been the happiest time of his life.

But Chiara was cooling now. There are limits to this feverish kind of equilibrium. Finally it was decided that Alistair and his wife would take separate holidays. The months of July and August would be spent apart. 'Are you sure you mean it?' I asked him. He had begun to phone me regularly, this time to tell me he had told Chiara he was leaving his wife. 'After all, that's not strictly true,' I said. 'You only decided on separate holidays.' He said he thought he meant it. Anyway the point was *he felt he had to make something happen*. It was an expression that stayed in my mind, an expression that gnawed. Perhaps because it was unusually honest. For thinking back now on the many friends I have who have divorced, or separated, or left each other and got back together again, or divorced and married someone else, it occurs to me that while most of them talk earnestly, sincerely, of their search for happiness, their dream of the perfect relationship, what really drives them is a thirst for intensity, for some kind of destiny, which so often means disaster, the desire to push things to the limit, to savour crisis, in ecstasy before, in tears and tranquillizers after. It's the same endearing perversity that found paradise so tedious that one way or another that apple just had to be eaten. Man was never innocent. Marriage was never safe. 'I have to make something happen,' Alistair said. In this finely managed, career-structured world we've worked so hard to build, with its automatic gates and hissing lawns, its comprehensive insurance policies, divorce remains one of the few catastrophes we can reasonably expect to provoke. It calls to us like a siren, offering a truly spectacular shipwreck. Oh to do some really serious damage at last!

But Chiara said no. Chiara said she didn't want to live with Alistair. She didn't want to risk the happy routine she had built up with her daughter after her husband's death. She didn't want to marry again, and in particular she didn't want, she said, to be responsible for ruining Alistair's marriage. They must stop seeing each other completely.

Alistair collapsed. The gods abandoned him. Intoxication was gone. He couldn't live without it. He couldn't live without joy, he said. He crumpled. His smoking shot up to sixty a day. He drank heavily. His wife was alarmed, became excessively kind. This infuriated him. He could barely speak to her. He could barely speak to the children. He could barely *see* his children. Unable to sleep, he dozed all day. His work went to pieces. And now he tortured himself with the reflection that if only he had asked sooner, Chiara would have said yes. He had tried to negotiate, to manage things. His procrastination had destroyed her passion. He should have trusted his instincts. Finally I managed to persuade him to see an analyst.

As I said, we live in Italy. It's a country where people divorce significantly less than in the Anglo-Saxon world, but perhaps have more affairs. It's a country which perhaps never believed that romance should be the lifeblood of marriage, or not after the children have arrived, a country where a friend of mine told me that at his wedding his grandmother advised him to try to be faithful for at least the first year. In short it's a place where people expect a little less of each other, and of marriage. Above all they don't expect the privilege of unmixed feelings. Hence a country where analysts give different advice.

The analyst told Alistair that only the wildest optimist would divorce in order to remarry, presuming that things would be better next time round. Why should they be? Was there anything intrinsically unsuitable about his wife, anything intrinsically right about his mistress? His problems sprang from his puritan English upbringing, from the fact that he'd never been unfaithful before. This had led him to attach undue importance to the sentimental side of this new relationship in order to justify the betrayal of values – monogamy, integrity – that would not bear examination. He had 'mythicized' it. What he must do now was take a few mild tranquillizers, settle down, and have another affair at the first opportunity, to which he should be careful to

9

attach no more sentimental importance than an affair was worth: some, but not much. And keep it brief. Meantime he might remember that he had an ongoing project with his wife. They had been through a lot together. They were old campaigners. Think of the practical side. Think of your professional life. He told Alistair that every family was also a business, or *hacienda* as the Spanish say, a family estate, a place where people share the jobs that have to be done.

Is such advice merely cynical? Or in a very profound way romantic? Old campaigners. Talking it over after Alistair had put in a decidedly lacklustre performance on the squash court, I felt it wise to agree with the analyst, at least about the ingenuousness of imagining things would be better next time. And I told him that during the Italian referendum on divorce in 1974 one of the arguments against divorce put forward by some intellectuals was that it would change the nature of affairs. I tried to make him laugh. You'd never know if your mistress didn't want to prise you away from your wife!

But visions of such consummate convenience leave little scope for myth and misery. Alistair had been *in love* with Chiara. He had *given his heart*. Such clichés do count for something, whatever an analyst says. Trying and failing one evening to have sex with his wife, unable to feel any stimulus at all, Alistair suddenly found himself telling her the truth. He didn't decide to tell her, as indeed he had decided nothing in this whole adventure. Everything had been done, usually after enormous resistance, under an overwhelming sense of compulsion. Perhaps this is the way with anything important. He told her the whole truth, and got his catastrophe.

Or so it seemed. The wife was destroyed. He had spared no details. She insisted he left. He did, discovering in the process what a large space home and children had occupied in his life. Most of this he struggled to fill with whisky and Camel Lights in a lugubriously furnished apartment in a cheaper area of town. Legal proceedings had just begun when Chiara came back to him. At this point there is a brief hiatus, since Alistair no longer felt the need to be in touch with me. He was so happy. So I heard later. He had won his dream. The hell with the analyst. The hell with squash. The wife, whom I had always liked myself, was more than generous with access to the children, Alistair was more than generous with money. He bled himself dry. All was well. Indeed perfect. It was about three months before I got another call . . .

I suppose what fascinates me about divorce is how tied up it is with our loss, our intelligent loss, of any sense of direction, of any supposed system of values that might be worth more than our own immediate apprehension of whether we are happy or not. We are not ignorant enough to live well, too arrogant to let old conventions decide things for us. Put it another way: for many, and especially for men, I think, who do not bear children and do not breast-feed them afterwards, the only thing that is immediately felt to be sacred, the only meaningful intensity, or the last illusion, is passion. D.H. Lawrence puts this very simply in *Women in Love*. Birkin says:

11

' "The old ideals are dead as nails – nothing there. It seems to me there remains only this perfect union with a woman – sort of ultimate marriage – and there isn't anything else."

"And you mean if there isn't the woman, there's nothing?" said Gerald.

"Pretty well that – seeing there's no God."

"Then we're hard put to it," said Gerald.'

Perfect union with a woman. Over beers again, depressed and tranquillized, Alistair was explaining how he thought he'd found that, until the night after love-making when Chiara casually asked him if he wanted to know the real reason why she had said no to his initial proposal that they live together. It seemed she had just started an affair with another man. With Alistair being married and mostly absent it was bound to happen. She'd wanted to see how it would work out with this man. Quite well, as it turned out. Though he wasn't at your level in bed, she laughed. Alistair hit her.

Alistair was now obsessed by the fact that there had really been no great love. Quite gratuitously, Chiara had exposed the illusion around which he was rebuilding his life. For now she said that she had had three or four other lovers during their affair. Why should she have put all her eggs in one basket and risk getting hurt? Alistair, who had never hit anybody, hit her again. The analyst explained to him that hitting her was his way of trying to preserve some sort of myth, albeit negative, about the affair, of trying to insist on its importance. Disturbingly, Chiara appeared to like being hit. She came back for more, told him more. It took them another year and two trips to hospital to stop seeing each other. It was always she who came back. Alistair told the whole story to his wife, who commiserated. They made love. They started seeing each other more often, but without interrupting the divorce proceedings. Alistair began a long series of affairs whose main purpose appeared to be to relive the passion of the earlier affair, whose main purpose, perhaps, was to rediscover the enthusiasm that had led him to marry in the first place.

Marriage and divorce are so tangled up with our sense of mortality. One lives such a short time, yet wishes to do everything, then to recapture everything. Start again, the springtime says. Unfaithfulness never fails to rejuvenate. But if we start again too often nothing will be brought to completion. And happiness? That long-term monogamy is unnatural is something that every male of the species has felt. Yet where would we be without some repression? The perfect union begins again. Another intimacy beautifully galvanized by the unbridgeable distance between men and women. A radical incomprehension. The children arrive. There are disagreements. The project falters. Our biology has little time for wholesome values and domestic routine now the reproduction is done. The sound of a river in the distance lifts your head from the loom. The sound of rushing water. Time to batten down the windows, sandbag the doors. Old campaigners will take their kids to cricket, or take up cricket themselves. Or piano. Or drawing classes. Or martial arts.

In a chaos of receding floodwater, Alistair surveys his rearranged landscape. He has the kids alternate weekends, eats regularly with wife and family. Sometimes it's hard to tell whether they're separated or not. The analyst has become a friend, plays squash with Alistair and swaps stories of affairs over beers. His main boast is three in three days at a conference in Palermo. The divorce has come through at last, and as divorcees will, both Alistair and his ex-wife assure me, perhaps a little too insistently, that this is indeed the ideal solution.

Fidelity

In the brief space the English leave between birth and baptism – my own in this case – our family was obliged to vacate the old rectory where I was born. The walls were crumbling with dry rot. Given the urgency of the situation, the local authorities generously provided a council house, a 'shoebox' as my mother always referred to it, in a working-class district of my father's parish. On arrival, all the neighbours dropped in to help, as they would in Northern England in the 1950s. My mother and father thus discovered that two other boys had been born and baptized in the same street only the week before, and that both had been called Timothy. This was irritating, since my parents had been planning to give me that name. Being clergy folk, they had their reasons: Timothy means 'honouring God'. On the other hand they did not want to be seen to be following fashion, and particularly not in a working-class district. Was there some famous actor called Timothy? Or, more likely, since this was Manchester, a footballer? Surely the whole street couldn't be reading the Pastoral Epistles? For a day or two there was dilemma and debate. But in the end my parents held firm and I got my name as planned. After the baptism service, as was the tradition, I was given a Bible, maroon leather bound with gold-edged pages, and when I

15

was old enough to read such things, these were the words I found my father had written for me, on the inside page, in his nervous, angular hand:

' "O Timothy, keep that which is committed to thy trust. . ." I Timothy 6, 20.'

The rotting house, the overlapping of fashion and devotion, my parents' steadfastness, my father's spidery dedication: only much later would it occur to me how appropriate all these details were. For the time being, as a child, I was merely disappointed to discover what a lacklustre figure my saint was. For Timothy performed no miracles. He didn't cause the dead to rise up, nor did chains fall from his feet in Roman prisons. No angels appeared to him. He was neither scourged nor crucified upside down. To a little boy, he hardly seemed worthy of his place in the Bible at all.

My parents were evangelical. They took their inspiration from the gospels and the *Acts of the Apostles*, 'Go ye into all the world and preach . . .' Thus it was natural that they should have missionary friends, and when I was ten or so a family we knew well and had spent our holidays with was martyred in Burundi. Taken in a rebel uprising, mother, father and two young children were offered a choice of denying their faith, or death. They chose death. We held a memorial service for them. And I remember asking my father then if Timothy had been a martyr. He didn't know. Not that my father was an ignorant man. Far from it. He had given up a career in engineering to take his degree in theology. But since, in the evangelical tradition, it is supremely to the Bible that one refers, and since in the Bible no mention is made of Timothy's death, it was natural that he would not know. Only shortly before my twenty-first birthday, leafing through the *Encyclopaedia Britannica* in a university library, did I come across the story: Timothy is reputed to have been martyred in Ephesus, of which he was the first bishop. Nobody took him or tortured him or insisted he deny his faith. He went looking for trouble, and this quite late in life. He was lynched by the mob on trying to stop the ritual orgies with which the Ephesians celebrated their goddess Artemis. It was about this time – my 'coming of age' as they say (whereas now one is merely ageing) – that I began to ask myself: who was this Timothy who so inspired my parents, ignorant though they were of his martyrdom? What did they mean by giving me his name?

Timothy was among the first of those who came *after*. This is one's impression, on reading the *New Testament*. Born a generation too late and four hundred miles to the north-west, in Asia Minor, he never knew Jesus, was spared the drama of Gethsemane and Calvary, never experienced the vindicating exhilaration of peering into the empty tomb. He was not in Palestine those forty days when the risen Christ showed himself to his disciples, nor in the upper room when the cloven tongues of flame descended on the apostles' heads. Unlike Paul, who more than anyone else bridges the gap between Christ's presence and absence, he was not granted the belated intrusion of the blinding light, the voice from the sky.

Timothy came after all that. The first few chapters of the

Acts of the Apostles are crammed with action. The church explodes into being. And Timothy was almost there. How many times, after Paul chose him as his missionary companion, when wrapped in their cloaks he and Silas and the great apostle gazed out from the prow of some merchant ship across the choppy Aegean, would he have heard tell of the early days: the three thousand converts that first morning of Pentecost; the demons cast out; the lame made to run; and that unique moment of communist Christianity when all the believers brought all that they possessed 'and laid it down at the apostles' feet, and distribution was made unto every man according as he had need'. Not to mention the more disturbing miracles: the terrible story of Annanias and Sapphira, who sold their property, said they'd brought all to the church, but kept some back. Unmasked, they simply fell down dead.

Listening to those stories, as the church spread and grew, the towns came and went, the ships, the caravans, as Paul preached and he and Silas and Titus followed, Timothy must already have been aware that the miracles were happening a little less often now, and that when they did it was always Paul who performed them. Did he already appreciate that after Paul had gone, there would be no more, that miracles and social revolution were not the order of every day? My father was a great admirer of Paul's. Indeed as he went about his pastoral business in an Anglican church whose complacent decay increasingly frustrated him, I suspect there was no one he admired more. He quoted from him constantly. Standing in the pulpit, his bald dome of a head glowing with excitement, robed arms upraised, he even looked like the figure of the apostle as shown in Bible storybooks, preaching to the sceptical Athenians perhaps. It once occurred to me that my father consciously imitated Paul. Yet he called me Timothy. Was the first great evangelist too ambitious a role model? Or, since it was perhaps we children who had prevented him from following a missionary vocation, could it be that he found it difficult to associate us with adventure?

Paul suffered from no such restraints. All too aware of the danger – what else had he looked for all his life? – he set off for Jerusalem, for gaol, the journey in chains to Rome and death. Paul was ever in the vanguard. But rather in the way some dashing entrepreneurs will set up a company and then bring in a manager to keep it going, he would send his closest disciples to watch over the churches he had formed. Thus Timothy was left in charge of Ephesus, one of the largest ports of the Mediterranean, bustling centre of trade and vice, 'Light of Asia', 'Highway of Martyrs', first in John's list of the seven churches, home, above all, of the great Temple of Artemis, with its image of the goddess that had fallen from the sky.

Was Timothy up to it? He was young still and his health was poor. Ephesus was a difficult place. Insisting on monogamy, the Christians had obliged converts to leave all but one wife. There were 'widows' who had to be looked after. And should non-Jewish Christians obey the old Jewish laws or not? Paul had encouraged Timothy to be circumcised, so as not to offend the Jews he must preach to. But to

Titus he had given different advice. Should a Christian slave obey a pagan master? Should those who worked full time for the church be paid, and if so, by whom and how much? Of course these were minor considerations beside the revelation of Christ's deity. Soon the Second Coming would put an end to such trivia. But in the meantime, disconcertingly, these matters had to be dealt with.

Paul wrote letters to Timothy to give him a hand. Keep the faith. Stir up your gift. A little wine with your meals is good for the constitution. Deacons, however, should not be heavy drinkers. Bishops should not be profligate. Behave. Let the women learn in silence with all subjection. Don't take widows into full-time church service under three score years. They may wax wanton. Reading this sensible advice, Timothy could hardly have failed to recognize that the headier days were definitely over. One even had to be a little cautious in one's evangelism now: 'Lay hands suddenly on no man,' Paul tells him. And, in general, beware. The latter days will be hard.

The latter days. Timothy stands in relation to Paul as the married man to the lover. He is in for the long haul. His sanctity is a work of unceasing maintenance, a coming to terms with routine. He is forever bailing in stormy seas. 'I have somewhat against thee,' writes Saint John to Timothy's church in Ephesus, 'because thou hast left thy first love.' Don't betray the promise of your youth, writes Paul. 'I give thee charge that thou keep this commandment until the appearing of our Lord Jesus Christ.' Until the Second Coming. But when would that be? Timothy had 'married' young, indeed was perhaps the youngest convert of early evangelism. He and his bride, the church, were to be together a long time. And while Paul wrote at length of deacons and bishops and widows' societies and wages, did Timothy begin to appreciate that he might be just the first of a thousand links in a chain set to stretch out across millennia to come, that Christ's triumphant return might be indefinitely delayed? Did he become anxious that he would not be able to keep the faith? Keep thy charge, writes Paul, safe in the knowledge that he himself was soon to be martyred in Rome.

My father preached at least once every Sunday. I know it became a burden for him to think of new things to say, to maintain the enthusiasm that caused one local paper to refer to him as 'our fiery northern vicar'. Was he becoming anxious about this when I was born? He had just turned thirty-four. First intimations of mid-life crisis? Was this what was on his mind when he chose my name? Was he warning me about what he himself most feared? How difficult it is to preserve the passion in the liturgy. As likewise romantic love in marriage. After all, I was the third child, and the last, my birth the moment, as any analyst will tell you, when a man senses the die is truly cast. 'O Timothy, keep that which is committed to thy trust . . .' Certainly, Paul's Pastoral Epistles mark the moment when one feels most keenly the shift from revelation to orthodoxy. History is turning out to be longer than expected. With time on their hands, men will be idle, they will talk, they will have new ideas, they will change things, subvert things. The whole verse reads: 'O

21

Timothy, keep that which is committed to thy trust, avoiding profane and vain babblings, and oppositions of science falsely so called.'

How to preserve the faith through the latter days? In the space of the few pages addressed to Timothy, Paul uses the word 'doctrine' thirteen times, more than in any other book of the Bible. And his prose is constantly congealing into creed. Sometimes it is almost a chant: 'God was manifest in the flesh, justified in the Spirit, seen of angels, preached unto the Gentiles, believed on in the world, received up into glory.' If time was to be long, then it must be frozen in 'sound doctrine'. Timothy's sanctity would be to achieve that, to turn passion into ritual. My father, though he had always criticized the Catholics for using Latin, was disturbed when the Anglican church finally gave up the use of its traditional 1662 Prayer Book. He knew how important an oft-repeated formula can be.

Even the most casual reading of the New Testament shows how it moves from revelation to repetition: the miracles, the acts, then the interminable exhortations; until, as though finally weary of all this, it finishes with the explosion of the Apocalypse, the Book of Revelation. That sanctity lay in suffering, Paul never tired of repeating. His own life would be a pattern for that. But what if, with orthodoxy successfully established, with half the kids on the block called Timothy now, persecution and all the intoxicating emotions it brings were simply not available? What if the routine of the latter days – watch and pray, watch and pray – begins to pall?

It must have been in the late 1960s that the tedium finally got to my father. The children were almost grown up, the world was in upheaval, and he was still there keeping a charge that never changed: the Parish Council, the Roof Renovation Fund, carol services and jumble sales. He was forty-six now. Faithful to his doctrine, with no intention of denying what he had always preached, he had the good fortune to find a new excitement within the Scripture itself. Much in the way that some in middle life will seek bizarre sexual stimulants with their ageing partners, my father discovered the charismatic gifts of the first letter to the Corinthians: tongues, prophecy, healing, exorcism. An American evangelist had come to town. We were in London now. There was a movement, uplifting meetings in suburban parks. My father was 'baptized in the Holy Spirit'. My mother followed, then the curate. They spoke in tongues. A flush of excitement galvanized the church. The congregation went out to preach on the street. There were great doings, many converts. And finally a demon was found too, as needs must be in movements of this kind. Why would a seventeen-year-old smoke dope and play wild music, if he wasn't possessed? Why was his hair so long, his beard so goaty? Was it possible his leg, lame from polio, could be healed? My brother laughed at them and hissed from time to time. He enjoyed pretending to be demonic. He enjoyed their outrage. Why would anybody, the faithful asked, give up a possible career in engineering to study at art college? This psychedelic stuff. My brother smoked No.6 and argued earnestly in favour of the Vietcong. It was 1968. Jimi

23

Hendrix was a genius. But my brother's lame leg, somebody said, could be a sign of Satan. For there was an immense desire in the church to have something happen now. It was all very well starting a charismatic movement, but something had to happen. On Christmas Day my brother locked himself in his room with a girl dressed in second-hand clothes and didn't come downstairs for his dinner. Why would anybody do such a thing if they were not possessed? The world must change, and must be seen to change, as it had for the apostles. Otherwise what were the gifts for? So, at last, there was an exorcism. And although one side was doubtless well-meaning and the other no more than normally rebellious, there was constraint and conflict and wild wild words. And the world did change: like the old rectory in Manchester where I was born, our family suddenly seemed dreadfully precarious, a structure that might tumble down and crush us all.

During that period of charismatic folly, which was so exciting, and so destructive, one of the things this fourteen-year-old Timothy did was to go out with parties of young Christians to picket places of vice. Our youth club burnt the records of a group called Black Sabbath, and in the evening we went to Soho and sang hymns outside strip joints and porno cinemas. We called them 'Soul-Searching Parties'. Generally the curate came along and someone with a guitar and we stood in drizzle under yellow lamplight asking people who smelt of drink if they were saved and encouraging them to think of the Odeon as evil. Amazingly, some listened. Most laughed. A few spat. But had we searched our own souls, what motives would we have found for our extraordinary behaviour? Were we moved by love of sinners? Or a sense of guilt that we had comfortable lives and had suffered nothing for Christ? Or was it just an ordinary eagerness for excitement and action, the way others brought up differently from ourselves went out looking for fights in football stadiums?

Thirty years after Paul had gone to his glorious death, Timothy was still holding the fort in Ephesus. He was old now and the church the established thing that Paul had so fervently wished. Timothy had kept the faith, assured an orthodoxy. But on 24 January in the year 97, or so the fourth-century historian Eusebius tells us, he had had enough. Timothy went out to picket the huge Temple of Artemis, one of the seven wonders of the ancient world, where the Ephesians were enjoying their licentious festivities in honour of the goddess. As the old saint stood there, definitely looking for trouble, perhaps outraged that poor health should hold out so long, did he intone, as we once did on the Charing Cross Road, the creed his religion had now become? Did he hurl one cosmology in the teeth of the other to have something happen at last? Or was he thinking wistfully of the youthful lusts that Paul had advised him to flee? Insulted, quite probably inebriated, the pagan Ephesians clubbed him to death. No doubt there were converts as a result.

Called out of this world as he is, the Christian is given the mission of getting the place straight before it is too late, not of loving it for what it is. Thus every Christian sanctity tends toward apocalypse, until, frustrated, it settles for immolation. For those of us who do not believe, those like myself who rejected what a father committed to their trust, that state of mind is nevertheless not incomprehensible. We have all had our passions and epiphanies, the intensities we have tried to cling to. So we can recognize the saint's peculiar heroism, the seduction of his folly: to hold a faith rigid across the decades, and then, when weary, to find some way of dying for it. We can see the glory of that, as the Christian no doubt must sometimes regret our own agnostic nonchalance, our enjoyment of 'vain babblings', of argument for argument's sake. But he probably also guesses that, however much at ease, the unbeliever will always hanker after revelation, as the Christian himself often wishes he could thrust its yoke from off his back. The family trauma past, half healed, my father settled down to the resolute and reassuring repetition of sound doctrine: matins and evensong, Christmas and Easter, and all the long rainy Sundays after Trinity.

Two years ago, I went into the British Museum, to see some fragments of the temple of Artemis at Ephesus, fragments of stone against which my namesake's head might feasibly have been bashed. They were not on display. And the Epistles to Timothy were not written by St Paul. So the experts tell us now. At most there are a few snatches from the apostle himself, stolen to give authority to some much later text still hammering at the gong of orthodoxy way into the second century. Thus Timothy becomes a representative figure of he who is to be admonished, exhorted, encouraged, he who grapples with fading memories, vigorous enemies, faint-hearted friends. And who could be more saintly than that? 'The cloke that I left at Troas with Carpus,' says one of the last fragments everybody agrees a historical Paul addressed to a historical Timothy, 'when thou comest, bring with thee, and the books, but especially the parchments.' How much more convincing and, somehow, encouraging these few lines are than anything in the Book of Revelation, than anything preached at evangelical meetings. Timothy, apparently, was the kind of person who could be relied upon to perform such a humble charge. Whatever his doubts, his state of health, that was one faith he would always keep: an errand for an old friend. It may have taken forty-one years, the birth of three children, but I begin to feel quite pleased with the name my father gave me.

Glory

Perhaps it's only when we set the greatest store by a seemingly trivial adventure that the metaphysical content of a certain variety of yearning becomes apparent. Yet why was I so upset that we could not start our walk from home? It would add an extra day, Fritz said. He could not get an extra day off work. Then the children were not eager to set out from home. They know the paths round here too well. Children can only be persuaded to walk if there is excitement involved. Hardship must be accompanied by glory. My wife drove us towards the peaks visible in the distance.

San Giorgio Veronese to Folgaria through fifty miles of mountains in three days. Myself, my friend Fritz, Michele aged eleven, Stefi eight. Italy's coldest summer on record. One Indian tradition puts down many of our anxieties to the fact that all the universe is nothing other than the dispersed and broken body of the first progenitor god. We benefit from his dissolution – we could not exist as individuals without it – and yet yearn for a lost wholeness. Could this be, I put it to Fritz as we faced the first bracing slope, why I was so sad about not starting from home? I had wanted – we struck up a cluttered gorge – the feeling of having covered the whole distance, of having put something back together, extended myself the whole way from home to Folgaria. Fritz was checking the batteries of his mobile phone which was to keep him in touch with the progress of the Tour de France. It was more likely, he suggested, that I was merely an obsessive. I attached my happiness to small and mindless achievements. He did the same on his bike when he had to keep the needles of the speedometer at exactly the same point for a certain stretch. Fritz, of German-American parentage, brought up in Italy, is a bike freak. Stefi said she was exhausted. We had been walking the best part of fifteen minutes.

The terrain above San Giorgio is a dull plateau of sparse grass and tumbling boulders. We worked our way up to its cracked lip, then over the edge where the land plunges down into the Valle di Rivolto. Here a sparse population still speaks the remnants of a tongue that is neither the Italian of the plain, nor the German of the high valleys, nor the Ladin of the mountains, but Cimbro, some bizarre linguistic fragment out on its own, which enriches these people, one supposes – they are very proud of it – and quite isolates them from the likes of Michele and Stefi who were now scampering down a wooded ridge to the Rifugio Pertica, because promised, in today's lingua franca, Coca-Cola on arrival.

Fritz went into the *rifugio*, a sort of big alpine hostel, but as yet there was no news of the Tour. For some reason his phone battery hadn't charged. He was concerned about his personal hero, Indurain. Apparently this extraordinary athlete had collapsed on some mountain stretch the day before for the first time in his career. It was important for Fritz's happiness that Indurain win the mad race a record sixth time. Stefi and Michele were also exhausted, they said, though the day's real challenge, the ascent of the Carega had yet to begin. They sat on a bench outside the *rifugio* and were allowed some chocolate for energy, but not a sandwich as yet. Stefi produced – I wasn't aware she had brought it – her small and favourite bear, Soletta, and this was at once endearing and annoying because I knew there'd be hell to pay if it got lost. Fritz explained that he had a magic drink with him called Energade which he would give in small doses to Stefi if she ever got seriously tired. It had immediate and miraculous effects, he claimed. People had walked for thousands of miles on a gulp of Energade and others had been brought back from the dead. A cycling product. Above us the clouds loured thickly on a wall of weathered stone where two adventurers were advancing inchmeal with pitons and coloured ropes.

How difficult it is to explain what happened next! What a wealth of detail – geographic, geological, chronological, meteorological – would be required to account for it all, what descriptions of mental activity in different minds, of group dynamics, different physiques! For even without engaging in the madness of counting the speckled stones beneath your feet, this broken body all about us is an extravagantly abundant thing. Every story told is carved from something so much bigger. Plus, of course, there was the business of the map. I have it here on the desk beside me, still wrinkled from the damp of six months ago . . .

Basically we were travelling north-east. We could reach this evening's hostel in about four hours by following a fairly simple path along a saddle and then steeply down through a narrow valley. Given the threatening weather, this would be wise. Fritz was for it, perhaps thinking that his next fix of Tour news would not come before our arrival at Rifugio Campogrosso. The children too were for it, already dreaming of dumpling stew, standard fare of all *rifugi*. But for me the whole point of our trip was to do the peaks. Where was the glory otherwise? It would be like the Tour de France without the Alps, I insisted to Fritz. Where the adventure? Where the profile of the thing? And in particular I wanted to do that first peak, the Carega. Because that was the one forever on the horizon throughout my fifteen years in Verona, emblem of those limits one never overcomes. Add my not reaching that peak to our not setting out from home and the whole trip was dust and ashes to me.

Indecision. Looking up, the mountain was lost in cumulus. The rock climbers' voices came faintly. Soletta smelt rain, Stefi said. Until, just at its most vulnerable, my project was saved by a gaggle of schoolchildren. They came up the track from Valle di Rivolto and the land of the Cimbri. Perhaps thirty ten-year-olds with teacher. Turning the hairpin, they seemed set to plod along the easy path. Immediately Michele rebelled. No way was he going to walk beside a school outing. Stefi too was indignant. The classroom had caught up with them. Their daily bread. 'To the Carega,' they shouted. Tackling the steep scree as colours faded in cloud, I thought: one yearns for wholeness,

31

yet wishes to distinguish oneself from the herd. Stefi's pigtails jostled before me, at 1,800 metres now. Still, I thought, this desire to recompose things does not seem alien to the push for glory. Rather part of it. How so? Then Michele discovered he had left his hat down at the *rifugio*. He swore and cursed with that impotent anguish of having lost something, being without something. Just when it seemed impossible, the path steepened.

And now came the agony of the map. These are ancient military relief maps over which some voluntary organization has inked in the paths, rather approximately, in what, printed, looks like mauve felt-tip. Handling the thing in the damp air, above the tree line, I suddenly noticed that at the very peak we were aiming for there was a gap between the paths approaching from this side and the paths beyond. Almost a centimetre. A valley perhaps? Or a crevasse, even? God's body truly severed here. I stared at the paper. Did this mean we would have to turn back and descend the way we'd come? In which case we would find ourselves far from our goal at nightfall. Without a bed. So as everybody pulled out jackets against the cloudy cold and Stefi began to whine that she was hungry, she wished she'd never come, and Fritz to comfort her, offering Energade, and Michele to mock and talk about courage and the difference between boys and girls, until Stefi refused to walk another step and sat down in miserable mist to eat her sandwiches on wet stones with the mountainside sheer above and below – all this time I was plagued by the thought that I was leading them into a trap, a dead end, which could prove disastrous, even fatal. You are always overstretching yourself, I thought. This is typical of your obsession with self-affirmation, your determination to impose shape on events. But here at the risk of your children as well. And in the most god-awful weather. Getting to our feet after eating, we were numb and sluggish. Yet in my eagerness to reach that peak I said nothing. Or rather, I talked non-stop, heaping encouragement on Stefi, calling her Crest-Strider, Mountain Girl, Peak-Dancer. What would Soletta say if you gave up before Michele? But the walk was ruined for me now, I thought, ever more apprehensive. We were four figures flagging in alpine fog. Please let it be all right, I muttered to no one in particular.

Or perhaps not. Mountain tops were ever the homes of the gods. Indra on Mount Meru. Zeus on Olympus. Jehovah on Sinai. Cloaked in cloud, the peak is obviously a place where two worlds traffic. So when we came out of the gloom on to a crest with the shrouded valley behind and a crystal landscape falling away in front, dizzyingly bright in its drops and pinnacles and wheeling birds, it shouldn't have been so much of a surprise to find a tall Madonna. White marble hands pressed in prayer, she stands on a red angle-iron frame above a heap of boulders held together by rusting wire. A plaque reads:

HOME FROM THE WAR
MARIO CARGNEL
HONOURS HIS VOW

GUIDE AND PROTECT ALL MOUNTAINEERS
AND BLESS OUR VERONA
1950

In difficulty, it seems, one begs a favour, makes a promise. Some give and take between gods and men is still imaginable on mountain tops. What could I offer, though, that might encourage the powers that be to bridge the map's little gap? Could I mention the trade, perhaps, in print? Put in a monumental word. Expose myself. So while Michele was facetiously taking 'bless our Verona' to mean his football club, which had just covered itself in glory by returning to Serie A, while Stefi shouted for joy because she had found her first edelweiss – or *stella alpina* as the Italians call them – I made the silent vow which now I honour: 'Please let the paths meet up. I will speak of it.' Almost at once the clouds came down again. But it wasn't a bad omen. Another half-hour trudging through the sky and we were on the peak. Carega. A barren cone of whitish shale topped by a rusty cross: 2,238 metres. The paths met up. Four hours later we were playing cards on bunk beds in the Rifugio Campogrosso. The children bragged, immensely proud. They had trekked a great trek, though Indurain it seemed was still more than a minute behind the pace. At 7.30 a smell drifted up through the pine walls: dumplings and stew.

Could it be some words release a smell too? Some names. Especially of places where much blood was shed. Waterloo, Verdun. And could it be that the perfume of those words is something like the fragrance that drifted up to the gods on their mountain tops when the sacrificial fires were lit? Stuff of metaphysical exchange. There are odd moments when thoughts cleave together, find each other in the dark and without the aid of logic, generating the curious sensation that the deepest things are about to be revealed. In any event, I was put in the oddest frame of mind when reading, over breakfast, the following sentence in my guidebook: 'For two and a half years the fighting never ceased: Pasubio was like an altar on which a burnt offering was sacrificed every day.'

Pasubio. We lost our way walking down from Campogrosso to Passo Fugazze and so didn't begin our ascent till nearly midday. Fritz, who is tall and looks ludicrously young, wore his peaked hat backwards like a cyclist. To be close to Indurain? About every two minutes he belched and blamed it on the pot of poor-quality coffee we had drunk. Michele giggled and counted the belches. In a sunshine that seemed to lie like bright enamel on every surface I held Stefi's hand as she explained to me the difference between elves and fairies. With the morning's warmth every bush was scented, and when I asked her what words she knew smelt nicest, the first she came out with were *stella alpina*, though that flower has no smell. Only later did I discover that the Austrian Kaiserjäger, who fought on the mountain above, had worn edelweiss badges on their caps.

At Passo Fugazze there was a café, but Fritz challenged us to reach the top before eating lunch, confiding to me that if we ate first the children might never make it. There were more than a thousand metres to climb. 'Impossible!' Stefi said. The slopes loomed awesomely. 'Which is why we must do it,' Fritz replied, solemn. Michele said he would only try if Fritz in turn tried to reach a hundred burps before the top. Fritz protested they were involuntary. In any event we climbed, he belched, zigzagging stoically, eyes fixed upon the ground where amazingly every step bestrides such variety of mosses and fossils and toiling ants and twigs and leaves and loam and stone, until towards one o'clock we topped a ridge and joined the Strada degli Eroi (Road of Heroes) coming up from Recoaro. In the sudden heat the children were desperately thirsty, as no doubt were the soldiers who once tramped up here before them.

Strada degli Eroi. Soglio dell'Incudine. My map gives only Italian names, admits no Teutonic overlap, despite the fact that this was once border territory, the Austrians struggling to hold together a disintegrating empire; the Italians convinced that the complete shape of their national identity was yet to be acknowledged. So while Fritz now took his turn at smothering Stefi in praise to make her walk, I asked Michele what he knew about this war. 'The brave Corps of the Alpini valiantly defended Italy from the Germans,' he said. Though actually it was Italy attacked Austria. But there seemed no point in bothering a boy with these dull details. For in everything one reads about Pasubio, and indeed the whole long front from Switzerland to Trieste, what remains is not the dubious politics, the inept strategies, but a cloying scent of sacrifice. These men fought for two and a half years in a savage, windswept landscape, hacked trenches in stone and snow, lived in caves and igloos at frightening altitudes, attacked machine guns in terrain where the only grave was a heap of shards. Did they really do it just for fear of their commanders? Or was glory a credible commodity for some of them? The supplies were brought on mules, I explained to Michele, who is not without a certain mulishness himself, meaty backside with fluorescent Invicta pack above. When avalanches blocked the road the soldiers starved.

My son decided to attach his own self-esteem to overtaking a young couple we could just see some way ahead. He marched off along this track blown from the rock face in just a few weeks it seems, now strewn with stones that fall from the overhanging mountain. At the *rifugio* above, amazed at her achievement, Stefi kept endlessly acting out her own earlier despondency, then consequent elation. 'We'll never do it' – face gloomy, shoulders slumped – 'We've done it!' – eyes radiant, a little hop and skip. 'We'll never do it, we've done it!' I took a photo of them beside the tricolour. On the wall behind, a plaque recalls General Graziani's famous message of 3 July 1916: 'I would wish to kiss you all one by one, officers, sergeants, soldiers, courageous defenders of Monte Pasubio, so that you might know how much the Italian people appreciate your spirit of sacrifice which, on July 1st and 2nd, was the salvation of this country.'

An hour later Soletta sat on the top of the Dente italiano looking across at the Dente austriaco. At 2,200 metres on an utterly barren plateau these two great rocks glower at each other like two sphinxes. Perhaps three hundred metres separate them, and thousands of ghosts. Neither side ever got the better of the other. With its rusting barbed wire and heaps of rubble smashed from the mountain by artillery fire, this is an excellent place for modern man to think his wise thoughts about the stupidity of war. Stomachs full at last, the children explored the tunnels beneath, poked beaming faces through gun emplacements. On a boulder big as a bus a notice explains that scores of Italians lie dead beneath. The Austrians dug a tunnel below them and packed it with 53,000 kilograms of explosive. Untouched, the place still keeps its sombre aura: of sacrifice, of vows never to be fulfilled, lives cut short, lavish wastage in a waste of stone. But Fritz was eager to get down to our next *rifugio* now. Fortunately Michele spotted Soletta. Then my silly suggestion that every new burp might shave a tenth of a second off Indurain's deficit had the desired effect. Amidst howls of giggles Fritz reached 220 as we trudged the long descent from the battlefield to Lanza. Where as it turned out we were to fight our own little war. Shown into one of three huge dormitories, it seemed certain we would have to share. But again we were determined to remain distinct, out on our own. Every time voices approached the top of the stairs and prepared to choose a dormitory, we would shout in Italian, English and German: 'Michele, must you fart so much?' 'Daddy, for God's sake, your socks stink!' Our lines held. Full of dumplings and stew, we slept alone.

Then something odd happened. In the middle of the night I woke, needing a pee, to find the room pitch black. Shutters tight, there was not so much as a blur of luminosity. I cannot remember ever experiencing such utter indistinction. With no idea where the light switch might be, I felt my way to what I hoped was the loo. In the end, to my shame, I pissed in a basin. There is a line in the book I'd bought – *A Year on the Pasubio* – that says, 'then, in the thick of the battle, I saw an Alpino come over the ridge to face the guns, rifle raised in sharp profile against the last light'. And for some reason, groping my way back through the shapeless, disorienting dark, I was overwhelmingly impressed by the idea of this stark figure carved against the sky, launching himself in mad assault. I thought how frequently that image of glorious profile stamps itself on the mind as the very essence of heroism. The men on the beach at Iwo Jima. Achilles before the walls of Troy. And on the brink of sleep I saw the connection that had eluded me the day before on striking up the Carega. Maximum distinction brings maximum precariousness. A brilliant flash, then, passing through the moment's awful violence, extinction. You are at one with the whole again, the vast broken body of the landscape. Only the name and gesture are left, releasing their special fragrance.

'Pasubio has become more famous than it was actually important,' remarks the contemporary historian who introduces *A Year on the Pasubio*. Being an entirely mental quality, surfacing in nothing more concrete than a word, glory tends to be belittled, or viewed with some embarrassment in a world where technique and her accomplice, information, are assumed to hold sway. The performance of different machine guns is earnestly discussed. And yet despite her new boots – Gore-Tex lined – and all the chocolate and mineral drinks, the creams for sores and plasters for blisters, young Stefi, I know, would never have climbed Monte Maggio on that third day had it not been for the flavour of certain words – Crest-Strider, Peak-Dancer. In a day that will remain forever epic, we first climbed up to Campiluzzi, then an awesome, exhausting eight-hundred-metre descent to Passo della Borcola and then heroically, at least for a little girl of eight, up a thousand metres again, into cloud and rain through boulders and torn roots, gorges and ridges and dizzying, dizzying vistas, to the peaks first of Borcoletta then Coston dei Laghi, Monte Maggio. These names! Threshold of the Anvil! Hill of Saints! Stefi, the ground may be hard beneath your feet, but all the same it shimmers with the sheen spun from our minds. Names do more to it than any artillery shells. When, utterly exhausted, we finally got down to the *rifugio* at Passo Coe it was to find it closed. Thus we trudged a further mile to Rifugio Stella d'Italia on the last hilltop above Folgaria where, amazingly, the wife of the *padrone* comes from Newcastle upon Tyne and cooks the most delightful English cakes. The children collapsed on soft beds in an ecstasy of anticipated swank. Oh, to tell their friends! But the TV reported that it was all up for Indurain. 'He'll retire after this,' Fritz said, suddenly grasping the whole trajectory of Indurain's glorious career. And he added, 'I did my best.' I consoled him with cheesecake and beer on the terrace.

On that first day on the Carega there was another plaque beneath Mario Cargnel's Madonna. It read:

Madonna of the Carega
Solitary – serene
In soft sunshine, in the lofty, bewildered silence,
In the shriek and crash of the storm
PROTECT, SUCCOUR
those who untiringly seek in the mountains
the way of the spirit
August 1971

Now, returning by train, I wondered whether we could be said to have walked the way of the spirit? Our trip had been: tired legs, blisters, damp clothes, heavy meals, beers, Coca-Cola, sandwiches, sweat, belches, giggles, problems with maps, coercion. Or alternatively: achievement, beauty, exhilaration, a vow, sharp images over huge drops, and the strong presence of those who went over the edge, on Pasubio. Or again – because of some mountaintop trade between earth and sky, mind and matter – it had been both. In any event, when my wife met us at the station we had plenty of stories to tell, their shape stronger with every telling as the dross fell away and the memory got down to the business of forgetting the unimportant, as a writer pares his essay to its theme. Soon the photos would be developed, capturing the most inspiring moments. And perhaps it was on my way to get those photos, a week or so later, that I saw – incredible coincidence, but true – a small tattered poster

41

announcing the death of Mario Cargnel. Aged eighty-one. All his *amici di montagna* were invited to the funeral. So it must have been him, the very same. And had that notice not been some months old, I might have gone myself. For his name now has a special fragrance for me, not quite of glory, but the gratitude of those who get back safely. Without wishing to live in a remote valley and speak Cimbro, wholeness can wait.

Europe

In the spring of 1993 I joined a coach trip from Verona to Strasbourg to present a petition to the European Parliament. My colleagues, fellow language teachers at the university, felt they were being discriminated against by the Italian authorities. The Petitions Committee of the European Parliament was an institution which might right such a wrong.

Twenty or so students came along with us, perhaps to support our cause, perhaps to get a couple of days' cheap holiday, perhaps out of a genuine interest in the workings of a major international institution. My colleagues, mainly male, represented pretty well every nation in Western Europe. There was even one Canadian. The students, almost all girls, were Italian. Against the swim of the sort of rhetoric that necessarily inspires such ventures, there were those who referred to the coach as the 'Shag Wagon'.

During the journey I read Plato's *Republic*. There was a loud stereo system picking up Italian radio, playing songs with refrains like 'You're a myth for me', or 'Pray for peace' or 'Not here, not here your smell this year'. The girls sang along. There were video screens which broke the monotony with a showing of *Dead Poets Society*, where a very American Robin Williams, effectively dubbed in accentless Italian, invited us all to forget our dull school-books and, with that old European Horace, *carpe diem*. 'Can't tell the dear young things more plainly than that,' one colleague remarked.

Towards ten we benefited from another miracle of modern communications, passing through the San Gotthard tunnel. But traffic was slow. It was that very special time in history when quaint rustboxes from those countries that never learned to build cars the way we did were monopolizing the slow lanes of every Western European highway. Czech and Polish drivers waved to us from behind broken windscreen wipers – it was still a brave new world to them – and when we stopped for coffee the service station was shrewdly exploiting fashionable notions of international fraternity by displaying the flags of all the nations they hoped to take money from. A poster claimed they accepted payment in six currencies. We bought *café au lait* and croissants, but then it turned out that even as we travelled that morning the Italian lira had plummeted. The Bundesbank hadn't done something everybody wanted them to. There was much talk of how unusual it was to have Germany rather than England playing spoilsport in the Community, and across plastic tables imitating granite the students felt they had been overcharged.

Then, back in the coach again, while crossing the Confederation of Switzerland, it occurred to me, between one page and the next of his *Republic*, that Plato did not believe in the realm of pure forms he spoke so much about. The weather was uncertain, with sudden gusts and squalls of rain. The girls sang along to songs that always seem to express either the pangs of love or the proper political ideals. Someone was waving to the Trabants. Someone was lamenting the fact that at twenty-two she still hadn't achieved an '*equilibrio interiore*'. And closing my Penguin edition to gaze at the philosopher's face carved in stone on the front cover, I reflected that nobody had seen more clearly than Plato that the world was a place of change and betrayal. Nobody had described its traps and quicksands, its cycles of decadence and revolution better than he. So that if he chose to deny this place any ultimate reality, I thought, if he spoke instead of an ideal, more real realm beyond, that was merely his way of expressing his outrage, expressing a mental space, a place of yearning that is in all of us: for things to be still, for everything to be settled, defined and resolved: our jobs, our loves, our lives. And it occurred to me that for those of us who live today in Italy, in Germany, in France, though not perhaps in England, that mental space is most frequently expressed in the word Europe, in our idea of a European Home where we will live in permanent peace and prosperity.

Passing Lucerne, the girl without the *equilibrio interiore* explained that she 'hoped she would resolve her problem before she was twenty-five'. How could she live after twenty-five without an *equilibrio interiore*? She was 'searching for something', she said. So a discussion got under way as to what exactly this commonly used expression 'searching for something' might mean. What was it precisely one searched for? Where and how? It was an inconclusive debate. Or rather one of my colleagues concluded that we frequently used all kinds of expressions suggesting paths of action that, on examination, turned out to be unavailable to us. A kind of verbal alchemy, he said, perhaps eager to impress a girl decidedly more interesting for her physique than her anxieties. And I thought how the whole of Plato's *Republic* involved the elaboration of a project which is unavailable to us, the whole book was dedicated to the erection of complex social and political machineries for realizing a situation of stasis and perfection that Plato himself *knew to be unrealizable*, even stating as much as he went along. What for, I wondered? Why this project and simultaneously the awareness of the pointlessness of the project? The coach moved through a wet landscape surreal with doodlings of afternoon neon. The radio played, 'You're a myth for me'. When we got to our suburban hotel it was to find the lira down by more than 5 per cent on the franc. Expenses would have to be revised. Much discussion as to who was going to share a room with whom . . .

Our case had to be presented with great delicacy, announced a lawyer who had come along to assist us. He stood up to speak at a long wooden table in one of those German restaurants where they encourage strangers to sit elbow to elbow as if proximity were the pleasantest thing in the world. For it turned out that Strasbourg is as much German as French, a typical border town where two cultures gaze at each other from close up and try not to be overly contaminated. Very aware of exchange rates, we ate dumplings in broth and boiled pork, and the point was, the lawyer said, that while, as foreigners, we were undoubtedly discriminated against *under Italian law*, which was illegal *under European law*, nevertheless *under the national laws of any other Community member* what the Italian state was doing to us (the imposition of temporary rather than permanent contracts) would have been *perfectly legal*, since laws were not so favourable to employees in other member countries. Not to mention Canada, the Canadian said.

What was required then, the lawyer said, though some of the students, and even one or two of my colleagues, were losing interest, was a double approach. To the non-specialist parliamentary members we were to meet we must stress the moral and emotional side: it was a battle for equality and human dignity we were fighting. To the members of the Petitions Committee, on the other hand, we must offer a meticulously technical presentation of the situation, since, overworked as they were, these people would be only too happy to find some legal hitch which would relieve them of any obligation in our regard.

A heated discussion then ensued, at least among the four or five people who were taking matters seriously, as to how best these two approaches should be articulated. Somebody said we could do worse than to remind the EPs of the three principles of *liberté, égalité, fraternité* on which all Western democracies and above all Europe were built. Somebody overturned a carafe of cheap wine. But I was struck by the fact that once again this was precisely the division that plagued Plato's *Republic*: between ideals and technique, between the initial vision of a state where to be just would

47

also mean to be happy, and then the hopelessly complex, indeed impossible mechanisms needed to bring this about. And when the lawyer said that we must under no circumstances allow ourselves to be drawn into a discussion of the fact that in other European countries the law was such that we would have no case to argue, I remembered that moment when Socrates warns that 'no one must know what is happening, if we are to avoid dissension . . .'

Waiting for the coach afterwards in the city's main square, the students sang and danced. This was the square where the historian Michelet tells how Saint Just had Elogius Schneider, ex-monk turned revolutionary, chained to the guillotine for having forced a girl to marry him or see her whole family summarily executed. Or so a French colleague was informing me, a woman in her mid-forties, lately divorced. She wanted to get away from the university, she said. She'd had enough. And watching the students dance and some of my colleagues dance with them, she said she was taking part in a competition which involved drafting a possible constitution for a United Europe. The prize was a year's research scholarship in Brussels. We admired the floodlit façade of the cathedral, the fine public space where the guillotine had once stood, and she said that one of the guidelines of the competition was that the constitution must enhance a sense of pooled sovereignty and common European identity. I wished her luck, while wondering whether the expression 'pooled sovereignty' wasn't paradoxical.

Then when the coach had taken us back to our hotel, a

group of diehards set out to find a bar for some late night drinking. The sour hotel proprietor gave directions that no one could understand. Under umbrellas someone sang an Irish song about English treachery. The Italian girls tried to learn it. Laughing, we got lost. There were those who cursed the French proprietor and indeed Frenchmen in general. A Dutch colleague and a Greek colleague separated from the group and appeared to be falling in love. But such was the determination to make the night memorable in some way, that on returning to the hotel towards 11.30 we managed to cajole the proprietor into reopening his own bar and selling us a generous selection of Euro-booze: Pernod, grappa, whisky. The Italian girls proposed a toast to Europe. In a low voice I asked one of our leaders whether he really believed in a United Europe as an ideal, or whether he just saw European institutions as a possible way of getting at our Italian employers, machinery for a tussle. With unexpected animation, he replied that of course he didn't believe in Europe. He couldn't give a tinker's curse, he said, about a united bloody Europe run by the German Bundesbank who raised and lowered their interest rates exactly as it suited them, God only knew what the lira would be worth tomorrow. And draining his glass in one gulp, he said quite vociferously that if the Petitions Committee or the European Court ruled against us, he personally would never mention Europe again. There were ringing cheers at this. But one of the Italian girls objected. She said Europe was our only hope, the European Community was our only chance of not being plunged into

49

another world war and of rivalling the American and Asiatic power blocs. A fierce debate ensued among bottles and glasses and giggles and spilt ashtrays. I recalled how Plato praised Socrates for being able to debate with the greatest subtlety even after huge amounts of drink. But our evening was a rather incoherent affair with the Anglo-Saxons complaining about the grappa and everybody but the Gauls somewhat wary of the Pernod. Whisky and English were the lingua franca and I stayed with those, until the French proprietor, like nations who sell weapons but don't like to hear them go off, came down to the lobby to complain that we were making too much noise.

The following morning I saw the European Parliament through a hangover. The building which houses the Community's democratically elected assembly, foundation stone of ultimate political unity, is set aside from the town proper, constructed on an artificial mound in its own abstract space. Outside is a paved esplanade and a line of national flags arranged in no particular order, presumably so as to avoid giving offence by suggesting a hierarchy. So many of our values, I thought, through what was really quite a severe hangover, have to do with seeking not to give offence through open reference to what we know to be most determining. As if Belgium and Portugal wielded equal influence with France and Germany! The students milled about taking photographs of each other by the flags while the Dutch and Greek contingents continued their canoodling. So many of our values have to do not only with not affirming our own power, I thought, but with denying the affirmation of power in general. Even the idea of being European has more to do with a rejection of nationalism than with any positive statement of identity. 'We Germans will feel safer from ourselves in a United Europe,' one of my colleagues had announced yesterday, eating his dumplings with the gusto of one pleased to rediscover home cooking.

But it was time to go in and present our petition. As we gathered in a knot near the main doors and waited for someone to distribute our security passes, there was a definite feeling of awe among colleagues and students alike, as of pilgrims, supplicants, newly arrived at a shrine. The great mass of the parliament building towered above us, tall panels of glass revealing that combination of polished wood, stone and stuccoed mural which expresses at once authority and luxury and ideals. And just as the flags outside were in no particular order, so the parliament building itself is circular, in order that no nation should feel they have been pushed into a corner. Padding over thick carpet and polished wood, the secretary who came to greet us on behalf of the Vice-President of the Petitions Committee explained that we had to go to the Left Hemisphere. One talked about the building in terms of the Left Hemisphere and the Right Hemisphere. Then, laughing at our amazement at the lushness of the place, she said that some referred to it as the most sophisticated brothel in the world.

What followed was rather an anticlimax. The centre of power turned out to be an elusive place. In a huge auditorium where interpreters looked down from glass cages above, ready to transform whatever was said into any

number of languages, our leaders presented our case to a
very small crowd made up for the most part of the students
we had brought along with us. But a dozen or so members
of the Parliament did turn up, and two were also members
of the Petitions Committee. Amplification and acoustics
were admirable. My headache wasn't improving. An Italian
member representing a political party in opposition said that
if his people got into power the kind of injustice we were
suffering would be a thing of the past. Because it was an
embarrassment to him to find his country perpetually in the
dock, he said. And I thought it strange how national pride
now has to do with being able to demonstrate how far one
has surrendered national interests. For the Community.

We ate in a clean canteen while the Vice-President's
secretary regaled us with stories. She explained to us how
the Parliament sat three weeks in Brussels, then one week in
Strasbourg. She laughed, mentioning the twelve heavy
trucks that each month set out from Brussels to Strasbourg
bringing with them heaps of documents and archives, only
to have to take them all back again a week later. She talked
about the problem of the thousand or so rooms of a certain
standard and quality which had to be kept simultaneously
available in both towns for elected members and their staffs.
Then she spoke engagingly of the politicians' sexual
peccadilloes. There were those who claimed that the
Parliament only moved back and forth every month so that
the men could get away from their regular mistresses for the
week. Everybody laughed and felt envious, and I remembered how in Plato's *Republic* Socrates suggested that those

who distinguished themselves in public life should be rewarded by being able to sleep with more women. This would ensure that the greater number of babies were born to the better sort. To which, in twentieth-century translation, Glaucon retorts, 'And quite right too!'

After an afternoon lobbying individual members, the evening was spent drinking again and congratulating ourselves that much had been achieved. Our jobs were safer, surely, than twenty-four hours before. Not to mention the fact that the international markets had granted the lira a breathing space. A Scottish colleague played bagpipes and the students danced again. Even the French hotel proprietor seemed in a better mood. Then, the following morning, in the coach on the way back, I opened Plato's *Republic* again and read those final chapters on the role of art in society. The poet would have to be banned from the ideal republic, I discovered, because, in his desire to entertain, he would always represent the lower emotions, the most scandalous scenes, and this would hardly encourage people to concentrate on leading a virtuous public life inspired by the best political ideals, an achievement that unfortunately tends to come across as rather dull in poetry. Thus Socrates. Thus Plato. And fair enough, I felt. For although I have never risen to poetry, the old Greek seemed to have understood my own anti-utopian approach well enough. Novelists can hardly be expected to construct narratives that honour political ideals, I thought. What had I been noticing about our trip, after all, indeed about the European Parliament in general, if not the self-serving nature of the one, the seamy

53

absurdities of the other. But stop a moment: assuming we did want to be as generous as possible to the Community, what could we honestly say?

I was born in the UK. In Manchester. Most of my adult life I have lived in Italy. Partly I still feel English. In particular, I support English football teams and prefer Boddingtons Bitter to Peroni. And partly I feel Italian. Italy is home, is work and wife and children. What I never feel is European. Yet I do worry about that. I do wonder if it mightn't be better if one could feel European, the way as a child one wished one could believe in God. And I remember now that when I visited the European Parliament I asked the Vice-President's secretary whether there was a chapel there. Perhaps because my father was a clergyman I wanted to amuse my sceptical self by seeing how they had managed to reconcile Protestantism with Catholicism. There was no chapel. But there was a 'Meditation Room', the secretary told me. I went there. It's a small space with a blue carpet and soft cushioned benches. There are no windows. One wall is a sheet of stained glass featuring an abstract design that might represent a huge enlargement of some kind of bacterium beneath a microscope. Raised on a low platform to one side, there is strange block of white laminate and polished Perspex, something that feels the need to be there, to focus the room, but is doing its best not to remind you of an altar, or a lectern, or a pulpit. And it occurred to me, here in the Meditation Room in the heart of our new Community, that the only thing one could meditate upon in such a place was how different it was from a chapel, how apologetic, how amorphous. As the only thing one had been able to think of, looking at the muddled line of flags outside the building, was the shedding of old nationality, not the affirmation of anything new.

Perhaps we in Europe today are European to the extent to which we desire to feel European and cannot. We cannot be enthusiastic. We know that our Community was built as a last resort, from the ashes of what was more than just another war, from too much knowledge. Unlike the United States of America, our project has no dionysiac spirit behind it, no fundamentalism. Or even excitement. Following the carnival of nineteenth-century nationalism, the nightmare of twentieth-century carnage, this new entity proceeds sceptical and crabwise from one compromise to the next. Its rhetoric is almost wilfully hollow. And this is its strength. Nobody is going to make a crusade of the European Community, though everybody fears they need it. It expands not by aggression but by surrender, the surrender on the part of each new member of that delirium of individual destiny which characterized our national pasts. And by a certain weary economic opportunism. One by one the surrounding states throw in the towel and join us. A project conceived during the most exacting of hangovers, Europe faces each new day with the wisdom of the morning after, determined never to touch strong drink again. We can thus feel fairly sure that, even if we must accept that it will never stir our souls, all the same we are hardly likely to be asked to die beneath its flag.

Perhaps no group has ever been more quintessentially

European than that hung-over multinational coach party of teachers and students returning from Strasbourg two years ago. My headache finally forced me to put down Plato's *Republic*. I watched the Italian girls trying to find comfortable positions to doze in, my colleagues chatting desultorily. We wished each other well, it seemed, within reason. 'Shag Wagon', though, was another utopia that had let us down rather badly, I thought.

Prajapati

Prajapati was alone. He didn't even know whether he existed or not.

I too am alone. It's fairly early in the morning. About 8.30. I am translating a book by an Italian writer called Roberto Calasso. The book is called *Ka* and amounts to a creative reconstruction of Indian mythology. The lines above are the first lines of the second chapter. This chapter deals with the god Prajapati, the oldest and first god, the Progenitor, and what is worrying me is that the Italian says, 'Non sapeva neppure se esisteva o non esisteva.' Should I have written, 'He didn't even know whether he existed or didn't exist'? Why does that sound rather odd to me in English, but not in Italian? Was the repetition of a key verb like 'exist' important? How far does the English auxiliary 'didn't' truly recall the verb it picks up? I can't decide. And frankly, although alone, I am very aware of existing. I tend to fidget when there's a problem, right hand thrust in my hair, toes twitching in sandals, because the day is hot, promises to be hotter. For a moment my body gets in the way of my mind. Then I decide that the best thing you can do with an intuition is go with it.

Prajapati was alone. He didn't even know whether he

57

existed or not. 'So to speak', *iva*. (As soon as one touches on something crucial, it's as well to qualify what one has said with the particle *iva*, which doesn't tie us down.)

'So to speak', *iva*. I like this word *iva*. I presume it's Sanskrit. This is the kind of thing Calasso knows about. You have to marvel at people like Calasso who read Sanskrit. Anyway, long live the apologetic in the face of the inevitably approximate. Or tentative. Or downright hazardous. Every translation should have *iva* as a postscript. Because now I'm very worried about the rather heavy weather I seem to have made of that parenthesis. The Italian was: '(Appena si tocca un punto decisivo è opportuno attenuare l'affermazione con quella particella, *iva*, Che non vincola).' *Punto decisivo*. Perhaps I should have written 'decisive', and not 'something crucial'. But is 'decisive' a true cognate of *decisivo*? Isn't decisiveness a quality of people rather than issues? Then I'm just admiring the elegance, the easy rhythm of that Italian 'attenuare l'affermazione' which I can't hope to emulate in my English, when I notice that, like many other words in the text 'decisivo' has been underlined in crude blue fountain pen, and this causes me to burst out laughing. My son should learn the word *iva* too.

How can I explain? Yesterday evening my wife told me in great annoyance that my ten-year-old son Michele had an exam the following morning (today) and wasn't even bothering to revise. I called for him to come and talk to me. A rather Dickensian scene. He explained that it was merely a question of the teacher's announcing a verb in some particular tense, person and case, and him identifying those variables and writing them down together with the infinitive. This was something that could present absolutely no problem for him. I tossed a few questions at him, though I always feel a little uncertain myself in the face of irregular Italian subjunctives and past historics. He seemed confident enough. To impress my wife I said, 'Michele, take any page of this book, underline every verb you come across and explain the cases to me.' Finding it open where I had left off, he studied this very page I am now translating. Then the phone rang, or there was someone at the door, and his work wasn't checked. Now I see that he had underlined the adjective *decisivo*. As a verb! He must have thought it was the first person imperfect indicative of some improbable infinitive like *decisere*. As *finivo* means 'I finished', or 'I used to finish'. Clearly he didn't bother to read or understand the thing. But then Calasso isn't easy.

I think of my son who at this very moment will be starting his exam in a gloomy classroom. Let's hope it's not decisive. There. The word can be used for events, not just for people! Yet I still feel the solution 'something crucial' was the right one. My son's self-confidence is perhaps inherited. At which point the sunlight enters the room and falls across my computer screen. This is always infuriating. I can't see anything. Since this room has no curtains I will have to pull the shutters to and work in artificial light for a couple of hours until the sun moves high enough for the light not to enter the room at such an oblique angle.

Closing the shutters, I remind myself that references to the sun's movement are a form of cultural inertia. But convenient. Like using 'he', 'his' or 'him' as pronouns for an ungendered 'someone', instead of the more 'correct' 'he or she'. And I reflect that the text I am translating refers to an unimaginable moment before there was an earth or sun, before there was any gender to distinguish, a moment when there was only this god, Prajapati, who didn't know if he existed (or didn't exist). In fact, if I remember rightly from my earlier and lamentably cursory reading of the book, it is in this chapter that the sun, or rather the Dawn, the rising sun, is introduced as a figure of awakening, mental awakening, of that which, by pouring in light, engenders distinction, difference, the other. Hence a female figure, and an erotic figure. One might take issue with that 'hence', but there is a link, apparently, between enlightenment and eroticism. For this is also the chapter that introduces the whole business of the creation of sex, and thus inheritance, of the variety that makes my son as sure of himself as his progenitor.

But am I? Closing the shutters on a dazzling hillside I am suddenly alone with the ghostly light of my liquid crystal computer screen. I have to reach under my typing table to plug in a neon light overhead. Neon is a noble gas, whatever that means. Was it present before the world was formed, when Prajapati was alone? If my son gets a bad grade in his exam, will my wife be furious with him? And perhaps with me too? My wife gets worked up about these things. Imagine if one could use the particle *iva* during the marriage service – 'till death us do part, so to speak'. Which again reminds me that this is also the chapter that introduces death. Sex and death must go together to keep the numbers balanced. *Iva.* Again that little particle which does not tie us down. 'Che non vincola' is better than 'which does not tie us down'. Terser, more reticent, it sits more snugly in a range of registers. But I could hardly have written, 'which does not bind' and left it at that: '. . . it's as well to qualify what one has said with the particle *iva*, which does not bind'. Could I? Why do so many English verbs seem to require an object? Does this explain our military vocation?

A fly is knocking against the neon. The Vedic texts and the Buddhist tradition teach respect for even the most minute manifestations of creation. You kill some tiny thing and discover you have committed an appalling crime, wiped out a brahman or something. Actually I'm not quite sure if I have this right. But that's the impression I got. The fly buzzes against the light, so that I have to make an effort to concentrate:

Prajapati was alone. He didn't even know whether he existed or not. 'So to speak', *iva.* (As soon as one touches on something crucial, it's as well to qualify what one has said with the particle *iva*, which doesn't tie us down.) There was only the mind, *manas.* And what is peculiar about the mind is that it doesn't know whether it exists or not. But it comes before everything else. There is nothing before the mind.

There, that was quick: four short sharp sentences with only minimum and fairly standard transformations of the sort you might make in any translation. 'La mente ha questo di peculiare . . .' becomes 'And what is peculiar about the mind . . .' 'esiste o non esiste' has come down to 'exists or not' this time. For some reason I'm not even worried about that now. For 'precede ogni altro' I've chosen 'comes before' rather than the cognate 'precedes'. I've noticed I have a habit of going for the Anglo-Saxon where I can. Is this a valuable intuition on my part, or just a bent I have? Perhaps I just want to make this text mine, swallow it up and regurgitate it in an entirely new form, the way these old gods always seemed to be swallowing up the whole world to spit it out again entirely changed, destroying to create – my lord Siva – sex and death? But if I stop over all these imponderables I'll never get anywhere. I must remind myself that one of the main reasons I'm doing this translation is to earn money to pay bills and feed my family. Attractive as it may sound, I don't live in a situation where 'there is only the mind'. There are also electricity bills, phone bills, Kellogg's cornflakes. The world of the other, the contingent other, is unbelievably abundant and solid around here. My children eat huge amounts of Kellogg's cornflakes, which, in Italy, cost a great deal more than they ought to. If I was happy about those lines being easy after all it was because they mean a little quick money in the bank. About five thousand lire a line if I'm not mistaken.

But then I notice that 'what is peculiar' about my son is that he has underlined the word *peculiare* as a verb. As if everything that ended in 'are' were an infinitive of the first type, like *arrivare*, or *amare*. How is he getting on? He will be bent over his classroom desk barely a mile from here, with the teacher squeaking out the words on the blackboard. And why does this fly never settle on anything so I can kill it? Frankly I don't give a damn about Buddhism and brahmans. Anyway I must have got that wrong. Indians must kill flies sometimes. All the time, quite probably. Though not cows. But just because of all those cows there must be a multitude of flies. And hasn't Calasso got it wrong when he says: 'What is peculiar about the mind is that it doesn't know whether it exists or not.' That can't be right. Nothing is more present to me, for better or worse, than my mind. Indeed it's a burden. Wasn't that the whole point of Descartes? I translate therefore I am. Unless Calasso is just making himself the mouthpiece of a different tradition. And in fact I realize at this point that I should have put the last sentence there in inverted commas. 'There is nothing before the mind.' It's a quote from somewhere or other. Calasso doesn't announce that he's quoting, he doesn't have footnotes, but here and there he puts things in inverted commas and if you want you can look up a list of sources at the back of the book and check page and line number to find where he's quoting from. Shall I? Turning to the last pages, I find that this is a line from the *Aitareya Brahmana* 2, 40 (I presume that means chapter 2, verse 40, like the Bible). And the *Aitareya Brahmana*, the glossary tells me, was reputedly written by Mahidasa Aitareya and is part of, or rather a canonical commentary upon, the *Rg*

Veda which means 'Knowledge constituted in verse'. Some-times I do wonder when I look at these references. I mean, did the original Sanskrit of the *Aitareya Brahmana* really have the same feel as that simple English, 'There is nothing before the mind'? Are the concepts 'nothing' and 'mind' and 'there is' the same in Sanskrit? Or even remotely comparable? Who knows. That present tense is curious, though 'There *is* nothing before the mind.' As if one were speaking of hierarchy as much as chronology. The mind's pre-eminence. *Iva*. It's funny that IVA is the Italian abbreviation for *Imposta sul valore aggiunto*, a European sales and service tax that the British call VAT. The fly settles on my keyboard and I try the business of clapping my hands just above it, which sometimes, by some odd law of physics, has the effect of drawing the fly up between the hands to be crushed there. But this one's a canny fellow. Perhaps what I really ought to do is find some 'official' English translation of these texts, the *Rg Veda*, and quote from there. But that would be madness, and not only from the economic point of view. I tried it with Calasso's last book, about the Greek myths, but many of the English translations of the classical texts Calasso quoted from were significantly different from his Italian version. He insisted he was right. He had worked directly from the originals. I decide to let 'There is nothing before the mind' stand, and I must admit I'm feeling more and more fascinated by that present tense, since it seems to change the sense of the whole sentence. Could it even mean 'in the way of the mind'? For example: there is nothing we experience in front of, or as it were obscuring, the mind?

That is an interesting concept, is it not? I'd hate to look up some English translation of the Sanskrit and find it said, 'There *was* nothing before the mind.' Mere chronology.

Prajapati. Mahidasa Aitareya. Calasso. Parks. Tongueless, Sanskrit, Italian, English. I think about this improbable chain of communication. Prajapati, the Progenitor. Surely his state of pure mind must have been enormously different from the buzz of my thoughts now, constantly distracted by that fly, wondering when the earth will have tilted enough for me to open the shutters and turn off the noble gas. Does the present tense, 'the mind *is before* . . .' perhaps suggest that Prajapati is always, that the origin is experienced over and over? The Vedic texts were collected in 1500 BC, thus, at four generations a century, there are something like $35 \times 4 = 140$ generations between Mahidasa Aitareya and myself. And anyway his was a commentary on earlier and older texts, impossibly distant now. Not that Calasso seems so very close either. He's a squat man, handsome in his way, in his mid-fifties, with a rather odd, very attractive voice, at once breathy and deep. He smokes Gauloises. I think of him poring over these dead languages in his study in an old *palazzo* in Milan some hundred or so kilometres from here. He treats me rather as a boy, a whippersnapper. Indeed I believe he sometimes refers to me as Pierino, a stock figure in Italian jokes, the cheeky schoolboy. There is no lift up to his third-floor flat. The walls are dusty with first editions. I have Penguin Classics. I use a computer (which reminds me that I should copy yesterday's work on to a backup disk). He writes in turquoise fountain pen on very thin, high-quality blue paper with a sort of rustly sheen to it. Just a dozen barely decipherable lines on each page, thousands and thousands of pages stacked away in file upon elegant file from parquet floor to cobwebbed ceiling. Clearly there's mania here, and preciousness, and vanity. Or perhaps he just finds he works best that way. Perhaps vanity is a help. It hasn't destroyed me. The problem is not being vain, but being at the height of one's vanity. And Calasso is, I think. I asked him once if he doesn't sometimes lose one of those sheets of paper, or forget where he's filed it. He said yes. He comes from a fairly well-to-do, intellectual Italian family. Apparently he was a child prodigy. I was born in Manchester, the son of an evangelical clergyman. At primary school I was captain of the football team. Sometimes, he says, he finds he's already written the very passage he's writing now. He thought it was only in his mind, still to be written, and instead he'd already written it. Calasso chuckled merrily about that. And remembering his chuckle, actually hearing it (*iva*), sitting here at my desk and kicking off my sandals so that I can get the cool of the ceramic floor, I realize that I am fascinated by models of the mind. By consciousness and representations of consciousness. Prajapati's, Mahidasa Aitareya's, Calasso's, they are all hugely different minds from each other and from mine. I was never convinced by Leopold Bloom. And I sense that translation has something to do with this, this constant attempt to grasp difference, to overcome it, if only for a few moments, if only on the slippery surface of a text, to appropriate, but also to expand, to be there in Calasso's study, understanding Calasso

understanding Mahidasa Aitareya understanding the *Ṛg
Veda* understanding Prajapati. Did they all find flies as
irritating as I do? Then the phone rings.

Somebody feels that, with the recent inflation in property
prices, my house is now under-insured. I get up and go into
the other room to switch on the answering machine. It is
not time for a coffee yet. Coming back it takes me almost
twenty minutes to add just five more lines:

> Prajapati was alone. He didn't even know whether he
> existed or not. 'So to speak,' *iva*. (As soon as one touches
> on something crucial, it's as well to qualify what one has
> said with the particle *iva*, which doesn't tie us down.)
> There was only the mind, *manas*. And what is peculiar
> about the mind is that it doesn't know whether it exists
> or not. But it comes before everything else. 'There is
> nothing before the mind.' Then, even prior to establish-
> ing whether it existed or not, the mind desired. It was
> constant, diffuse, undefined. Yet, as though drawn to
> something exotic, something belonging to another spe-
> cies of life, it desired what was definite and separate, what
> had shape. A self, *atman* – that was the name it used.
> And the mind imagined that self as having consistency.

I am really not happy with any of this. This abstract stuff
sits so far from the genius of English. The best part of the
book will be when we get down to the stories. That 'prior'
niggles: 'prior to establishing,' sounds awful. I hate the
word 'prior'. But what can I do? The Italian uses *prima*

twice. '"Non vi è nulla prima della mente". E prima ancora di accertare se esisteva o no . . .' (at least my son didn't underline *prima*, didn't think it was the third person singular of an improbable *primare*). But can I repeat 'before'? Can I write, ' "There is nothing before the mind." And even before establishing . . .' I think not. Too clumsy. I shall have to stay with the somehow bureaucratic 'prior'. And how odd it sounds to write, 'the mind desired', without establishing what it desired. Without an object. Once again English wants to tie us down, so to speak, with an object. A verb like 'desire' seems incomplete without one. How is it that Italian seems so relaxed about splitting that appetence from what it seeks, about enjoying verbs without knowing what they're up to? Can one desire without an object of desire? Here I can't play the game I did with the object-less *vincola*, turning it into 'tie *us* down', where that first person plural pronoun really stands in for anybody and nobody, the trick of an object that remains entirely vague. For the whole point of this particular sentence seems to be the irony, or paradox, of Prajapati's desiring when nothing else existed for him to desire. I ponder a while over the infelicities of what I have written, then follow an old maxim of mine established in the early days of translating manuals for quarrying equipment: when in doubt, hug the original, the way the girl in the folk-song hugs her fairy husband who turns into a thousand different beasts and monsters before declaring his final and more favourable identity: 'the mind desired'.

Oh but I do hate all these cognates! 'Existed' for *esisteva*, 'desired' for *desiderò*, 'diffuse' for *diffusa*, 'undefined' for *indefinita*, 'exotic' for *esotico*, 'species' for *specie*, 'definite' for *definito*, 'separate' for *separato*. When the text gets abstract, Anglo-Saxon caves in to Romance and the Latin cognate rules supreme. I look up 'diffuse' and 'undefined', first in the dictionary then the thesaurus, in the hope of discovering at least a choice to make, but there is nothing. 'Widespread' and 'vague' carry entirely different subtexts ('the mind is vague'!). And speaking of vagueness, I should never have allowed my son to go to school this morning in his present state of preparation, or rather lack of it. He underlined both *diffusa* and *indefinita*. Two adjectives for verbs. I am beginning to dread his return at lunchtime. He will surely have failed. My wife will be upset. Calasso, I reflect, doesn't have children. He doesn't have a son. So these are not the kind of worries that will be hovering about his text. Unless, when he deals with a word like 'progenitor' it occurs to him precisely that he does not have children.

So the undefined yearns for the defined, the mind for substance; the same way perhaps that I feel eager to get to grips with this translation, to have it crystallize in English. Around ten o'clock is one of my most fertile moments. And I'm aware that Calasso is fascinated by that opposition, defined, undefined, by the way the whole of experience might be described in terms of the constant exchange between those two categories. Translation too is this, leaving the definition, the apparent definition, of the original, going through a state of indefinition, perhaps more original, in the Prajapati sense, than the original, a state

69

where ideas are somehow held wordless, or almost, in my mind (I wish I could decide whether those ideas actually do become wordless) thence to reappear, gradually recompose themselves, from fuzz to clarity, or almost, in my own language. It's a process perhaps not unlike that by which Captain Kirk is each evening of this month being beamed down in a repeat series on Italian TV where he discovers, to my surprise, but not my son's, that somewhere in the transporter he has changed language, he now speaks fluent Italian, though oddly his lips move to American speech patterns. There is always something disconcerting about translations, an unsettling strangeness that survives from the original, a xenolith perhaps, or a trophy brought back from a conquered tribe, some object whose purpose nobody understands. In any event, I like this idea of the undefined becoming anxious to embrace the definite, perhaps in order to define its undefinedness. And how fascinating then that this embrace is called the 'self': self is a collision of diffuse consciousness and definition in a person, and hence, necessarily, not quite defined, not quite undefined: Calasso in his study, me in mine, which has now become my son's bedroom too since he is growing too old to sleep with his sisters and there is no other room in the house.

Do the Sanskrit *atman*, Calasso's Italian *sé* and my English *self* all mean the same thing? The fly has now found where a small glob of apple-pie filling was dropped on the desk beside the keyboard. I can't help snacking when I have my ten o'clock coffee. And if I said before that I was never impressed by Leopold Bloom – I mean by the representation of Bloom's consciousness, his *atman* – it's because it is too verbal, or rather, because it supposes Bloom verbalizing everything. Whereas so much of consciousness is not verbalized. And if I choose this moment to tell you that, tell you that I think that, it's because it occurs to me now how much is going on that I haven't told you about as I translate this page of Calasso, how much that I haven't verbalized at all. There's the irritation of my skin sweating through my T-shirt against the seat back. There's my brother's elegiac painting of ice on the lake at Fontainebleau. It hangs below the neon light. My eye lifts to it now, to its extraordinary play of ice and grey and hinted pink, embers of sun made visible in a tiny column of smoke, or mist, which illuminates the whole, all framed in sharply polished brown. There's the whirring of a cicala outside which sits behind the buzzing of the fly like bass behind treble, occasionally amazing with sudden silences. And otherwise there are a thousand objects in the room. Intermittently I'm aware of them, but without verbalizing. Do I even verbalize my concern for my son's exam? Isn't it rather there like a mood, a taste? How much of thought is words? No, these things it seems – I mean the verbal, the non-verbal – they cut across each other, rub off each other, like two currents forever meeting or passing one below the other, one above the other, or the way brown river water from the air has still kept its colour far to sea in the endlessly repeated embrace of defined and undefined.

'And the mind imagined that self as having consistency.' The Italian *consistenza* has only one sense, that which describes a substance, not the additional English sense of constancy through time, constancy of purpose. Yet I see no other way of translating this. In any event, the key word here perhaps is 'imagined': 'the mind imagined'. But 'imagined' in the sense of 'falsely supposed'? that is: 'the self didn't really have consistency, but the mind supposed it so'? Thus the mind in error? Or 'imagined' in the sense, 'the mind brought the self into being with this consistency, willed it thus'? The mind as creative power. There are times, I feel, when my translation is as unstable as my son's grasp of grammar. I'm sure I'll change it all when I revise.

I clap my hands again. Again the fly escapes. Every text, original or translation, is carved, conjured out of this precariousness: a thousand sensations and pressures, a surface buzz of words – consciousness – and then the extraordinary purposefulness of the mind, seeking, desiring definition, in the order of words on a page, something it can imagine as having consistency. Would I have translated this paragraph exactly the same way a year ago, a year hence? Would the syntax have tightened a little on a winter's day? Did the ringing phone, my son's exam, turn a definite article to indefinite? What if they paid me better, if I could afford to spend another hour over this sentence or that? Imponderables. Calasso himself has the irritating habit of sending me corrections to passages I have already translated, some obvious enough, but some quite inexplicable, more to do with the reflection of light off a glass cupboard perhaps than any flaw in the original text.

Light. I go to the window and throw open the shutters.

No defining dazzle floods in. Amazingly, everything has changed. Leaden clouds are thickening with thunder. I have visions of a power cut wiping out the memory. Could I translate the paragraph again, exactly as it is? Quick: F9. Save the morning's work. Then it occurs to me I could phone Calasso and ask him whether, when he discovered he was writing the same passage twice, it was indeed the same, the very same words, or significantly different. What did his chuckle mean, more than a year ago now? Was it his awareness that the same passage was not the same at all: the initiate's secret that much of his text is quite arbitrary? But you don't just phone Calasso for a chat. Calasso is a busy mortal man. His time is preciously portioned out for his various projects. I feel I must finish at least this paragraph before treating myself to coffee.

> Prajapati was alone. He didn't even know whether he existed or not. 'So to speak', *iva*. (As soon as one touches on something crucial, it's as well to qualify what one has said with the particle *iva*, which doesn't tie us down.) There was only the mind, *manas*. And what is peculiar about the mind is that it doesn't know whether it exists or not. But it comes before everything else. 'There is nothing before the mind.' Then, even prior to establishing whether it existed or not, the mind desired. It was constant, diffuse, undefined. Yet, as though drawn to something exotic, something belonging to another species of life, it desired what was definite and separate, what had shape. A self, *atman* – that was the name it used.

73

And the mind imagined that self as having consistency. Thinking, the mind grew red hot. It saw thirty-six thousand fires flare up, made of mind, made with mind. Suspended above the fires were thirty-six thousand cups, and these too were made of mind.

Fires, cups, thirty-six thousand: how well these extravagant images suggest the red-hot mind. The fruit of long research, no doubt. Obscure references, the psyche's mad abundance. Calasso can only write a limited number of these books, I tell myself. They require so much work. And they will all bear his unmistakable imprint, the grain of his *atman*, the particular pattern in which his consciousness crystallizes out. Whereas anybody with a good knowledge of English and Italian could hazard a translation. Could it be that mine here is only the first in a long chain of other attempts? Thirty-six thousand, even. Why not? What if this passage became a set text for some exam or other? And I imagine each individual translator beset by flies and phone calls and fickle weather, or paralysed in public examination halls, floundering through a wash of non-verbal material, then a maze of syntactical and lexical alternatives, towards the mirage of the definitive version . . .

In the hope that my translation of this passage was and will remain the best, I revised it some months after writing that initial draft (quoted above) on a train journey from Reggio Calabria to Bari. An editor is yet to have his say. Then Calasso will make an objection or two. This article, I might add, begun the morning my son failed his test on

Italian verbs, was entirely rewritten between reading two chapters of Siri Nergaard's excellent anthology *La teoria della traduzione nella storia* while sprawled beneath an orange-and-green sunshade on an Adriatic beach. Everything around me that day was scorching hot, as were the thousand cups of coffee I have consumed in translating the 527 pages of *Ka*, one of five books written, miraculously, by the Italian author and publisher, Roberto Calasso.

Maturity

'That is no country for old men,' wrote Yeats. I am in my daughters' bedroom. About once a month, Sunday mornings, I order a clean-up. One must begin with great impetus, and even then there is little hope of finishing. The toy boxes under the bunk bed. The clutter under the cot. The big wicker basket to be opened, if you can ever sort out the junk on top. Shelves groan under a terrible promiscuity of papers and pencils and books and dolls and bricks and counters and playing cards and – oh – here's one of Barbie's ski-boots, here's the pirate's hat! Shall I try to stick the pterodactyl's beak back on? 'Stefi? Stefi!' But my daughter is pulling things out of the wastebin. 'Not my drawing of the Hunchback, Dad! Not my *Little Mermaid* catalogue!'

Appetence was what Yeats meant of course. There will come a time when it is no longer appropriate. Not that I'm at that stage yet, but the children do help one to sense that all too soon . . . 'Mine!' Little Lucy appears and tugs at a horse's leg. Stefi disagrees. The hamster scrabbles when his cage is kicked. 'Kids, cassettes in the pile on the left, books on the pile in the middle, dolls' clothes in the plastic case. Lego things . . .' I look up to find my son leaning against the door grinning. 'You're ancient, Dad.' This is prelude to his asking for money. He wants to go fishing. 'The salmon-falls,' I remember Yeats, 'the mackerel-crowded seas'. 'You're going cuckoo,' he tells me. 'Take a break.'

I would have been thirteen or fourteen, I suppose, when I began to feel sorry for my parents. It was a new pathos and worked on me strongly. My father started to take a nap after lunch. Sprawled on his armchair he would remove his dog collar, loosen his trousers. A thrombosis in her leg, my mother had begun to diet. Shoulder pains forecast whatever weather we would be under. Apart from church functions, they rarely went out in the evenings. He read his Bible commentaries, she knitted. Come 10.30 they were yawning over cocoa.

To me this inertia seemed unforgivably melancholy and I was angry with them. Life must be whirl and appetite. Life was thirst for life. Not only beer, and hopefully girls to laugh with, and older people's cigarettes, but books and music too. I read, as I ate, voraciously. But out of the earshot of my mother's clicking needles. They were a clock marking wasted time. I could never have imagined there might be more going on behind her concentrated frown than in all the busy pubs of North Finchley.

Now the same gap opens between myself and my son, who doubtless feels I'm just deciding whether to be mean or not. There is a complacent plumpness about his twelve-year-old flesh, a radiant unselfconscious confidence. 'Out with the loot,' he demands. My own skin is looser now beneath the razor of a morning, and shrinking slightly to the skull. Already there are evenings when he stays up later than I do. Handing him a note, I think, as he surely cannot, of the gesture of passing a baton. And simultaneously, something else occurs: that such thoughts are compensation. Not life straightforward and simple, but vitality savoured in reflection, his eager bustle with jacket and tackle held for a moment in the pupil of my now not quite so blue eye. Then my reflection on my reflection.

Stefi sorts a muddle of books. Lucy's come in such various sizes as makes shelving problematic: pictures of teddy bears among animated toys, Little Red Riding Hood before the trip down the digestive tract. All hauntings and fantasies are here externalized, as if the brain were not aware of its horrors till objectified in the wicked witch, whose broomstick you can touch with your fingertips and find it tough and wiry. Stefi's more sober volumes restrict themselves to a line drawing perhaps at the beginning or end of each chapter. Her favourite now is *The Hobbit*, in which a middle-aged fellow is persuaded to act as if he were young and sprightly. To kill a dragon of course. And if my son does not read quite as voraciously as I once did, still his appetite resembles mine when I retreated from my mother's ticking needles. No longer witches and goblins for him, but real-life adventures. Into the pocket of his jacket he slipped a copy of *The Flight of the Intruder*. Vietnam fighter pilots roar over narrow streams, waiting for the trout to bite. Where there is reflection on the war, he skips, he tells me, as I once skipped perhaps half of *Vanity Fair*. But this morning the post told me an American publisher had rejected my latest novel, because too internalized. 'It all happens within the mind,' they complained.

Perhaps it is not surprising that a culture devoted to youthfulness should have begun with an explosion of huge and hugely detailed novels: Thackeray, Dickens, Eliot. The young in one another's arms. The fury and mire of human veins. Plot is the most obvious fodder for literate appetence. As young men see only the most obvious qualities in a girl, only the most obvious outcomes. And even those great novels are now abridged. 'Where's the other cassette of *Great Expectations*, Stef?' 'There's only one, Dad! It's not a long story.'

We're trying to match tapes and their cases now. Sherlock comes sheared of much of Watson's admiration. Winnie the Pooh and Piglet are spared even Christopher Robin's affectionate condescension. Pinocchio has lost his pathos. It's as if an infant's antics had not been gathered in his mother's eye, or my daughter plaiting her hair without me to see and contemplate. Present without past or future. Provincialism of the immediate. If there were once two birds on the Vedic Tree of Life, one eating, one watching him eat, these days they are both busy pecking the plant clean.

How long is Stefi's attention span? She keeps getting distracted. Wasn't this drawing good! Mum and Dad are queen and king. How did this puzzle work? She turns the pages of *The Three Musketeers*. Then enjoys a moment of righteous anger, because Lucy is taking the clothes off the dolls and tossing them in the air. 'All our hard work!' she wails. Then says proudly: 'You know I'm getting hair in my armpits, Dad. Soon I'll be a woman.' Children are eager to grow up, of course, I tell myself, dividing crayons from felt-tips, but this is neatly severed in their minds from the idea of ageing. They will never be more than twenty-five, I think, sitting Barbie and Ken together by the goldfish bowl. After which everything around them will urge them to stay that ideal age. Reflection is not encouraged, I reflect. The preface to the only copy I could find of Chateaubriand's *Mémoires d'outre-tombe* tells me that they have cut all 'the writer's meditations on the destiny of man'. And kept in: 'accounts of facts, descriptions of men and houses and palaces, dialogues'. In this way it becomes obvious what a modern writer he was. A children's writer almost.

Our culture has an implacable aversion to age, something that goes far beyond its ugliness and infirmities, beyond the mere selfishness of those who have no time for declining parents, beyond the understandable vanity that would reverse hair loss or lift a drooping bosom, beyond the fear of death, even. People seem to accept that they have to die, but resent the idea of ageing. Yet the process is well under way. Already one has to be careful about what one eats. Already one loves young women without being in love with anyone in particular. Suddenly, appetite is no longer quite part of me, or yes it is, but a potential enemy too. A scission is taking place. Do I have to decide what side to stay on? What is the way forward now? Throw oneself into appetite or renounce it. Stay in 'that country' or pack my bag against eventual departure? Where to? Sail the seas with Yeats and come 'to the holy city of Byzantium'? City of art and intellect. Of hammered gold and gold enamelling. What kind of a trip would that be? Stay young, the bias of my culture tells me. Look around.

Lucy has gone into a trance. The sun has turned a corner and the little girl sits staring into a beam of light, hands uplifted, faintly gurgling. Children do this till they're about three, I've noticed. As if still intermittently in contact with something that came before, something other. Then the concrete world overwhelms them: the brightly coloured toys and tinkly music. Fish, flesh and fowl. Stefi has sneaked off. For all the help she was. I can hear her skipping rope slapping on the terrace. Finding that a hump beneath the carpet is in fact a copy of something called *Shakespeare's Stories*, I am suddenly reminded that probably the first hero to perplex my adolescent reading was Hamlet. Why all that paralysing reflection? Get on with it! Until for O level I read somewhere that Hamlet was not so young as modern performances depicted him. Yorick had been dead twenty-three years, and Hamlet remembered him well. Some scholars even placed the prince at pushing forty. On the way to my parents' torpor. All was explained. Yet I could never beat my father at chess.

'I shall never tire of underlining a concise little fact,' says Nietzsche, 'namely that a thought comes when "it" wants, not when "I" want.' As if the more thinking that goes on in a head, the less easily one can talk of 'that famous old "I" '. Or you could say that the more powerful the mind becomes, the more it is like a series of highly polished surfaces, ever more capable of receiving and reflecting, back and forth among themselves, whatever is around. But less

81

interested in action: in fishing or skipping or revenge. Instead the mind is thinking of itself thinking of fishing, skipping, revenge. As when Michele looks at me, asking for money, and I remember myself looking at my own father and imagine Michele's son looking at him and indeed all the sons who will soon be fathers looking at their sons. There is a point where, if not quite confused, passive and active seem somehow less important, interchangeable in time. Deep down, Hamlet knows his problem is not cowardice, or even thinking too much, but rather that thought is his chief pleasure. He wants to be left alone to soliloquize in peace. Without these ugly problems to resolve. 'May not imagination trace the noble dust of Alexander, till he find it stopping a bung-hole?' ''Twere to consider too curiously,' the practical Horatio objects, 'to consider so.'

Then I'm just beginning to enjoy thinking about Hamlet, whom I haven't thought about for years, and to reflect that it is perhaps this that our culture will have no truck with, the idea that the greatest pleasure might come, not from consumption, or action, or doing good or passion, but merely, wonderfully, from the mind's play with itself, from withdrawal, when I find no fewer than five chocolate-cake wrappers under Stefi's pillow. For heaven's sake! 'Stefi! Stefi-i!'

My daughter's way is to burst into tears and confess at once. Unlike my son, who lies blind. 'Horrible Daddy,' Lucy pummels my legs, 'to make Tefi cry.' The older girl whimpers: 'Michele said to do it!' This is always her line. A reversal of the original garden scene. And she takes me upstairs to show me even more wrappers tucked away behind Michele's tape recorder. 'But where did they come from?' There are more than twenty in all. Eventually it turns out that Mummy's money drawer has been rifled. My children have started stealing.

The garden was paradise before appetite came on the scene: with it sin, then history. And some would have us believe that withdrawal from appetite can restore paradise. 'Meanwhile the mind from pleasure less,/ Withdraws into its happiness.' Thus Andrew Marvell, approaching Byzantium in a leafy Yorkshire grove. And I remember when my father read his dusty commentaries – and how fat they were – he would occasionally say 'Ha!' out loud and snap the tome shut to stare at the Victorian mouldings round the ceiling. I felt I would die of shame if ever my friends saw how ridiculous he was. Only recently, reading Coleridge's remark that his pleasure in reading was as much the enjoyment of observing his own mind at work as his passive response to the content on the page, did I appreciate what Dad had been up to. He had retreated into that world where 'the mind is its own delight', a place one can only begin to glimpse at a certain age perhaps. My father would have been as lost as Hamlet, I reflect, had he found himself dealing with a murderous stepfather, an adulterous and complicitous mother. Certainly he was always annoyed when the phone rang. Forced to engage, the paradise of reflection becomes the paralysis of inaction. What do I do with stealing children? Stefi is already sobbing into a cushion, moaning that I will never trust her again. Her whole life is ruined.

How kind modern movies are with the likes of Claudius and Gertrude! I have seen three or four recently which dwell with affectionate indulgence on appetite in old age. Allen's antics. Octogenarian nuptials. We are to arrive at death in the bright blaze of unjaded appetence. Falstaffian, but slim. Engaged too. Busy. Still contributing to neighbourhood improvement projects. 'He was an active member of the Rotary Club to the very end.' Whereas Hamlet was appalled. 'You cannot call it love . . . at your age.' And on dispatching the ever busy, well-meaning old Polonius: 'Thou wretched, rash, intruding fool, farewell!'

'Getting down to doing something,' remarks Emil Cioran, no less savage than the Prince of Denmark and definitely on the same wavelength, 'means getting down to the false and fictitious.' And again: 'The capacity for renunciation constitutes the only criterion for spiritual progress.' But how can I? I have so much I must get down to. There are still three drawers in the dresser to sort, the shelves above the bed, the heap of clothes behind the door, a great mountain of fluffy animals. And now this awful business of their stealing. 'What are you going to do?' my wife demands, red in the face from her morning run. And of course it is wise of her to keep fit. I am thankful she looks so young. Perhaps maturity is some imperceptible moment when two worlds are in perfect equilibrium. Those birds exactly balanced on opposite branches. The eater, the observer. Mind powerful enough to catch and reflect every gesture of still active appetence. Unwilling to retreat into itself as yet, but wonderfully enriched by the secret that such pleasures lie ahead. Oh the books, the explorations, the new intensities! Oh, the letting this world go to rack and ruin! 'You'll have to do something,' my wife repeats.

And now we're sitting together over pasta. On the terrace. The bright Italian sun. Above a garden too parched for Marvell's ecstasies. Too naked beneath the glare. But with a bird or two all the same to rustle the twigs. A white cat to make the shadows conscious. Michele is describing the fish that got away. The way a thought sometimes is the more present for having escaped you. Trembled the hook then lost, before you could even guess what species it was. Unless golden, perhaps. Of such a form as Grecian goldsmiths make. My wife is staring at me over her glass.

'You stole some money, Michele.'

How lush it all is now. His quick glance at Stefi. Her eyes going down to her plate. His appreciation that the game is up. Her chest heaves. His lips harden in anger. Betrayed! Then quiver. He's wringing his napkin in his hands. Lucy, oblivious, spears her pasta, shouts 'Tina' at the cat. And the explanations begin, the back and forth. Recrimination, confession, punishment, forgiveness. Not much communication though. 'I wish I hadn't, Dad. I wish I hadn't.' How Dickens would have relished the tears gathering in his shrewd blue eyes.

People say children keep you young, but that's not true. The person who stays young is the person who leaves his children to start again, or is ever busy elsewhere. Rather say, children give one the opportunity to become old, reflecting them, reflecting on them. For the lives of the young would be nothing without the old to observe them, as some once believed that all our lives were nothing unless gathered in the infinite mind of the divine. And it might even be there is perhaps some existence of universal mind beyond the mercurial fragments trapped within these globes of bone. Who knows? Our inability to locate it in the universe can mean very little if we still haven't found the thing inside our skulls. 'Of course we love you,' my wife is saying. Is that the force Nietzsche spoke of that pops the thoughts into our heads? So that we ingenuously claim, 'I think'. As the meal progresses – my stern voice, the wine, the children's sheepishness, the cheeses, a dog barking, the fruit, the promise to repay – it's as if I heard, very faintly my father cry 'Ha', and the knowing click of my mother's needles. After which we retire to ping-pong where the ball whizzes back and forth between our bats. Back and forth. And Stefi says: You never finish tidying my room, Dad. You always say you will, but you never do.

Ghosts

'Our Christ is not a dead Christ,' my father repeated. He was objecting to the Catholic cult of the crucifix. 'The cross is an empty cross. Our Lord is all powerful.' So he believed in the charismatic gifts, and above all in healing. But not in appearances of the Madonna. What kind of miracle was that? And why were Catholics so ready to see their madonnas cry? As if the poor woman were still contemplating her son's agony. A clergyman who once had responsibility for a large graveyard, my father told good corpse and coffin stories: the one that floated in the rainwater and had to be sunk with stones; the decomposed foot seen poking through the wall of the grave. He laughed, for death had long since been vanquished. And when they sent me to a high-church school, I was told not to turn to the east with the others when we recited the creed. 'Christ does not haunt a particular spot,' my father said. Dimly, I became aware that Catholicism was about the endless contemplation of pathos, Protestantism its sensible exorcism. Hence my shock so many years later when my mother told me – and I believe her – that she had seen my father's ghost.

Ghosts: by broad day they can scarcely hold our sceptical attention. We see through them. But at night, around the uncertain edge of dreams, and when the wind nags, there are few whom an odd sound will not thrill with apprehension for that long anticipated meeting: a dead father, a dead lover. The bibliography to Daniel Cohen's *Encyclopaedia of Ghosts* remarks: 'There are hundreds of books of "true" ghost stories, mostly, it seems, from England. These should be read strictly for entertainment.' But be sure they will come back to haunt you later. After pooh-poohing the whole thing, the *Macmillan Encyclopaedia* is obliged to conclude its entry on ghosts with the laconic reflection: 'Hauntings continue to be reported.' There is more here than meets the eye.

Every ghost story is two stories: the story of how the ghost came to be a ghost, the story of our encounter with the ghost. Or rather: pathos and our attraction to pathos, the siren song of others' sufferings, metaphor of all melodrama. 'The clanking of chains grew louder and louder' – it was Pliny the Younger, writing in the first century AD, who first offered us this scenario – 'until there suddenly appeared the hideous phantom of an old man who raised his arms and shook his shackles in a kind of impotent fury.' But Pliny's ghost did not speak. For whatever it is that leads them to their pitiful need for manifestation, ghosts rarely seem able to talk about it. Aphony, after all, is a common product of trauma, and what more traumatic than dying? Trapped inside his awful last experience of life, the shackled ghost beckons. Night after night. The house he haunts is soon abandoned. Until, in this particular 'true story', the impecunious philosopher Athenodorus, taking advantage of the low rent, has the courage to follow the phantom. A shallow, murder victim's grave is discovered, the corpse still manacled hand and foot.

Speechless, the ghost is extravagantly theatrical. He does not dress casually. Flicking through the first pages of *Haunted East Anglia* – for every English county has its crop of ghosts – I underline the following: 'the figure of a man was seen, dressed in soldier's uniform of the Napoleonic Wars' – 'the form of a punt, and a figure in a white dress, standing in it, poling the craft along' – 'the woman's dress was long and loosely flowing . . . the early sunlight caught and lit a quantity of gold jewellery' – 'wearing a metal breastplate and round steel cap' – 'wearing a long dark dress with a frilled apron and a small white cap perched on her dark hair' – 'wearing fawn coloured breeches, leggings and a checked coat: on his head was a hard pork-pie type of hat'. If this sounds like a shopping list for BBC Costume Drama – 'strictly for entertainment' – one should remember that the Madonna likewise is never without her blue gown, nor Christ his stigmata. And even my father, who appeared twice, though only once to my mother, did so in his white surplice that was such a bind to wash, and his black cassock that always hung behind the door to the vestry.

What are ghosts about? The dead body is walled up, chained, beheaded, burnt, poisoned. In any event trapped. Passing through walls, transgressing the barrier of those two dates that form a prison cell for all of us, the mute ghost wants to lead us back there, to insist on the past. He is a conservative fellow. Or, worse still, the ghost is he who walled up another, chained, beheaded, poisoned another. Unpunished for his murder of fellow actor Thomas Hallam, Charles Macklin long haunted the corridors backstage at Drury Lane. A thirteenth-century rabbi who killed his wife and burnt down his synagogue is still to be heard wandering around the Tudor building erected on the scene of his crime. Sinned against or sinning – and most of us are both – the ghost is appalled, by his relationship to a particular action or situation. Fixed there, unable – like so many in life – to change hair or dress or address, he stays home and haunts.

My father neither killed my mother nor burnt down his church, but one evening he wandered into the kitchen to eat cold meat from the fridge and said: 'I suppose this monogamy business is all well enough, our life.' Officially, though, he began to die the day after he married myself and my wife. This was the last religious ceremony I ever took an active part in, or ever shall. My older brother, perhaps disturbed by my parents' attempts to keep him in the Christian fold, had married far from home, in a town hall in Maryland, without a word to them. Aware of their sorrow, my more cautious choice, though unbelieving, was not so much to conform as not to disappoint. Undoubtedly it is these ruptures between what we are and what we do that come back to haunt us later. But when my father said he would use a microphone, I objected. He had never used a microphone when I attended his services. Technology seemed in bad taste on that particular occasion; it would amplify my own imposture. Stoically, not quite himself, my father gasped through the ceremony. The following week they were trying to decide whether or not it was too late to operate.

By far the most moving ghost story, to my mind, is

Ambrose Bierce's 'The Moonlit Road'. The husband wishes to see if his beautiful wife is faithful. He says he is away on business, but returns in the early hours. A figure slips out of the house. Mad with rage, unable to catch the fellow, the husband rushes upstairs and, without a word of explanation, strangles his wife. She returns to haunt him. He loses his wits and his memory. Bierce tells the story in monologues. Neither protagonist understands what has happened, or is privy to the knowledge of the other. The now decrepit husband longs for what he imagines as the release of death. The only thing that survives his amnesia is a dream vision of the night he saw a figure leave the family home, then went upstairs and killed his wife. Speaking through a medium, the dead wife tells how she awoke in terror, heard footfalls on the stairs. They receded. Just when she thought she was safe, they returned, louder and heavier than before. A moment later fingers were on her throat. Far from being released, she desperately seeks to manifest herself to her husband, as a gesture of love. And in so doing destroys him.

But who was the figure who entered and left the house? 'There are times,' the husband says, 'when I cannot persuade myself that it was a human being.' As if there were three ghosts in this story: the sorrowing wife, eager to repair a cruelly interrupted intimacy; the husband, haunted by his own inexplicable crime; and this mysterious figure who flits across the space of incomprehension between man and wife, phantom personification of that scission between what we are and what we do, source, in any event, of those deep misunderstandings that haunt us all.

One of the things that frightened me as a child at my prayers was that one might die and discover that all one had believed in was untrue. My father was now a sick man walled up in his cancer. Already he was experiencing the loneliness of the ghost, who almost always haunts alone. Certainly, despite his faith, he suffered the horror of the spirit become aware of those incongruous shackles that bind it to the blighted flesh. Certainly, he had his regrets, which, like anybody, he was eager to settle. My brother was sent for. I was asked if I would renew my faith. I would not. The ghost of misunderstanding strutted through the vicarage walls, effectively aphonous.

Modern technology has made it notoriously difficult to have certain psychic experiences. Candles no longer flicker, and just as streetlamps have robbed us of the stars, so the click of a switch will quickly turn a phantom back into a dressing gown. Ironically, though, great strides have been made in multiplying the numbers of the living dead. What need have I of ghosts when my amnesiac grandmother at ninety-eight is drugged into perennial decay, a dusty spectre of lost vigour? Thus X-rays and chemotherapy gave my father eight months to practise the ghostly pallor, the gestures of impotent fury. Is it surprising, then, that his first appearance as a spirit actually came some hours before his death? A close friend and fellow clergyman phoned my mother to say he had seen my father at the rather grand ordination service he had been attending: bishops, canons, deacons and archdeacons. Sitting in the stalls, fully robed, my father followed the ceremony throughout, only to disappear amongst the congregation when the friend tried to approach him after the blessing. Fittingly, flittingly, he died upon a Sunday.

One encouraging aspect of many ghost stories is the power they allow us over the world beyond the grave. For so often the end of the story is also the end of the haunting. In Pliny's account, Athenodorus follows the ghost to the scene of his murder. The skeleton is released from its chains and properly buried. It haunts no more. In *Healing the Haunted*, Dr Kenneth McAll, Christian psychiatrist, recounts perhaps forty personal adventures of freeing ghosts from whatever fetters them to their weary routines. Recognition, proper burial, prayer and exorcism are his tools, and no spirit anywhere is safe from them. The busy doctor sees off a pack of Norman knights, dogs, cats, unborn babies, and even the drowned and murdered slaves apparently responsible for the sad notoriety of the Bermuda Triangle. Compulsive repetition at last interrupted is always the happy ending. But intriguingly no mention is ever made of where these ghosts are released to: heaven, hell? What kind of release would that be? For all the cartoon efficacy they concede to Christian symbolism, ghost stories definitely haunt the margins of established religion. Offering no easy afterlife, their genius is to be most reassuring precisely as they find expression for what is most taboo: not death, but our wish that death really be death. 'Beneath it all,' wrote Philip Larkin, 'desire of oblivion runs.'

In the months he was dying, my father never sought healing through the laying on of hands. This is curious, since he firmly believed in such things. Perhaps he feared it had been his charismatic fervour that had led to the painful conflict with my brother, proved the mocking elf that draws us to destruction. If cancer is partly the result of stress, my father had had his fair share of it. The other explanation is that, despite his sense of outrage at what was happening to his body, he was not unready to make an end: perhaps precisely because of that outrageous gap between felt identity and the enigma of one's life. He may have had quite enough of figures who slip in and out of the house at night.

But did Father really know he was dying? Certainly the doctors were careful never to use that word. 'It's so discouraging.' And the literature on the subject makes it clear that none of us can really fully imagine our own extinction, 'and whenever we make the attempt to imagine it,' says Freud, 'we can perceive that we really survive as spectators.' In which scenario we might understand the ghost as simply a failure of the imagination. 'There creeps in,' writes F.H. Bradley, 'the idea of a reluctant and struggling self, or of a self disappointed, or wearied, or in some way discontented. And this is certainly not a self completely extinguished.' What could be more of a failure of imagination than that grisly repetition beyond routine: same clothes, same gestures? The nights immediately following his death, my dreams of my father were always of a corpse that turned out to be reluctantly, discontentedly alive, dead but frighteningly not so. Was that why on the third day, the day before the funeral, I asked the undertaker if he would open the coffin and let me see my father one last time? He said: 'You don't really want to see your father. He is dead.' 'Blessed,' remarks one of Samuel Beckett's characters, performing a healthy amputation on a verse from Revelation, 'are the dead that die.'

It's interesting, in Pliny's tale, that his murdered ghost does not seek revenge, but only the propriety of proper burial. The end of a ghost story is ever a return to propriety, that is, extinction. And propriety was very much on my mind as I leafed through brochures of wreaths, photographs of rose trees. What to do with the dead? Returning to the crematorium to pick up the machine-ground remains, I was surprised to find them being given to me in a colourful plastic box more suitable, one would have thought, for ice-cream than ashes. 'Was it a difficult death?' the woman asked – she had known my father well, in the way of business – and in the car, his car, though he never drove because of poor eyesight, I imagined tying the seat belt round the box, since my father was always scrupulous about wearing his belt. 'I've put them (it? him?) in the bottom drawer of the dresser,' I told my mother, not wishing her to be distressed by the garish box. Clearly propriety was yet to be established.

Was it in this period before the ashes were finally laid to rest that she saw him? Certainly that would fit in with the folklore on the subject. Obliged to leave the vicarage, my mother moved to the other side of London. It would be inappropriate to haunt their old parish where a new incumbent must establish himself. A stranger in a strange church, there came the moment, before the eucharist, when people are invited to turn and embrace those beside them.

No one turned to my mother. She was bereaved and alone, the ghost of herself. Upon which my father appeared in his robes and embraced her and she knew that all would be well. She could not say how he appeared, nor how he disappeared, only that he did so. On a windless day, she scattered his ashes in the Thames at Kew.

'I have related this in the past tense,' says the husband in Ambrose Bierce's 'The Moonlit Road', 'but the present would be a fitter form.' The images that haunt him know no solution. In this regard my father showed a generous propriety, appearing but twice and requiring no exorcism to be released. Unless, that is, one reflects that turning up in one's robes is not the only form of haunting. In so many ways life's continuance is a living death. We are haunted by ghosts of lovers past. By the country we left. By our father's religion. Our parents' faces loom in the mirror. Our cheeks shrink onto their bones. We chide our children with their gestures, at once haunted and haunting. My son's 'Oh damn' is in perfect imitation of my own. My eyes, my mother's, stare out of his young face. Will he one day have to write about, write out, me? I'm not averse to cold meat in the evening. And on opening the fridge I hear, quite distinctly, my father's words. Perhaps I spoke them myself. There's an odd distance, it seems sometimes, between the person I feel I am and the life I live. Will death cure us of this? 'All's well,' abbreviated Robert Lowell, 'that ends.' Well, it doesn't.

Charity

I am frequently moved to tears, but rarely give to the needy. On the phone a man is telling me that his budget is huge, hundreds of thousands of dollars. Is he to spend it merely telling people that Benetton sweaters are prettier and better than everybody else's? How dull! It's much more interesting for him to get involved in sponsoring a conference against famine in the world. Or this thing down in Corleone that he is trying to persuade me to go to. One is helping people is the point. And if that sells sweaters as well, then all the better. 'I'm pretty sure we could get your article published in *Espresso*,' he says. I decline.

Has the attitude of devotion to the human race somehow substituted for wisdom, and even common sense? On my desk there is a fax from a TV company. They have been commissioned by BBC2 to make a series called *Writers on Rwanda*. 'By presenting the situation through the words of writers we can say more controversial things than when expressing a view directly.' After each programme they will announce a phone number for people to call to pledge their gifts. 'We know you are already very committed,' they concede, but all the same they would like me to comment on my reactions to watching the disaster unfold on television ('your feelings of hopelessness, yet questioning of the appropriateness of some of the footage'). I remember at Sunday School they showed us slides of starving children in Rwanda and Burundi. I had a Church Missionary Society savings box in the shape of a mud hut in which I inserted a tenth of my pocket money. It is interesting that someone can write a word like 'committed' without feeling they need to specify to what exactly. Yet despite this assumption of some mainstream I belong to, it is also evident that anything I say will be 'controversial'. And desirably so. It occurs to me that lucidity is an ancient enemy of devotion. Paradox is the territory of faith.

When the guy from Benetton phones back I pluck up the courage to tell him I didn't like their recent poster of the three bloodied human hearts, all identical, with the legends black – white – yellow over them. Nor the guy dying of AIDS. Nor the bloodstained clothes from Bosnia. 'But these were important in raising people's consciousness,' he says. 'I found them unattractive.' 'You can't deny they were powerful images. They have impact.' I tell him I prefer the impact of beautiful girls wearing bright Benetton sweaters. When I accept the TV company's offer to write about Rwanda, but warn them that my piece will indeed be controversial – I will be explaining why I tend to steer clear of visual depictions of famine and genocide – they do not take the trouble to reply.

One of the things I remember perplexing me on Bible study evenings in my father's church was that verse in St Paul's eulogy to charity where he says: 'And though I bestow all my goods to feed the poor. . .and have not

98

charity, it profiteth me nothing.' This seemed contradictory. How can one give everything away, without charity? Then someone explained that 'charity' meant 'love' not charity as we now use the word. Only later did I start asking myself why, in that case, the Bible hadn't used the word 'love'? Since it used it when Christ says 'Thou shalt love the Lord thy God with all thy heart, and thy neighbour as thyself.' Without being a student of Greek, I suspect that Paul was aware of a charity that is profoundly uncharitable. 'If I knew for a certainty that a man was coming to my house with the conscious design of doing me good,' writes Thoreau in *Walden*, 'I should run for my life.' And he coins the splendid expression: 'kindness aforethought'.

The chief of publicity at Benetton is a namesake of the great saint: Paolo. And he confesses to being a practising Catholic. He has sent me copies of a magazine called *Colors* (funded by Benetton) and also of the Benetton catalogue. Each issue of *Colors* focuses on some remote location and concentrates on showing how warm and human ordinary people's lives are. The catalogue depicts locals from the same locations wearing Benetton outfits. All the better, I get the impression, if the place is a trouble spot, or in the news for some reason; its notoriety is thus harnessed to the Benetton trademark. Over his robes, an elderly Palestinian sports a fashionable pullover. A young Cuban taxi-driver has a new orange T-shirt. An obsessive levelling process haunts these pages. From all over the world people are quoted, unsurprisingly, as having the same fundamental aspirations: on one side of the photo a description of the Benetton garment, on the other the wearer's appeal for education, love, peace. . .

On the phone again – he is nothing if not insistent, but always pleasantly so – Paolo says it has to do with people understanding that the world isn't just one market, but also one family. I suggest: 'As when the Pharisees asked Jesus, "but who is my neighbour?"' Paolo hesitates. I explain: 'That was when he told them the story of the Good Samaritan.' 'Right.' 'But the Samaritan,' I object, 'didn't dress the man he'd saved in a Benetton T-shirt and use him for publicity.' Paolo is inured to this kind of attack. 'From an intellectual point of view that may be a reasonable scruple,' he agrees, 'but as I see it, it's just a typical smart person's excuse for doing nothing. You keep your hands clean, but you don't help anybody.' He adds: 'Anyway, a guy left to die in the dirt would hardly have objected to a few photos being taken, if that was what it took to be saved.' This is fair comment. I imagine the convalescent victim smiling in blue shorts and primrose shirt in a scene-of-the-crime shot beside the Jerusalem–Jericho highway. And I wish him well. Though the Samaritan with his Nikon has shrunk in my estimation. He has lost his dignity. No, more than that: he has lost his right to inhabit the mind as an archetype. Into the brief silence Paolo says: 'Anyway, I can now offer you ten million lire.' Six thousand dollars is more than I have ever been paid for a brief newspaper article. I accept.

The things that move me to tears are almost always things that surprise me, that have no designs on me. I'm doing the dishes and the radio says that a man has jumped from the sixth floor of a hospital with his handicapped child. I close my eyes and take a deep breath. But it need not be an event of such pathos. The line of a song: 'Hearts and bones, they won't come undone.' That always gets me. But it need not be sentimental either. A fragrance at twilight, the outline of a figure hurrying into a house. There is an overwhelming consciousness of our shared destiny at such moments. A sudden invasion of sympathy and yearning. Thankfully, it doesn't last. Nor does it prompt me to sign cheques for charitable organizations. But it has this in common with the Samaritan's encounter: the element of contingency. Nothing suggests that this generous man was on the lookout for a mugging victim. And once I did help a tramp having an epileptic fit in Hyde Park. Now, however, I am on a plane off to join a group of people – the Benetton team – who make it their business to hunt out objects of sympathy.

Of course I have demanded freedom in whatever I write. Of course they have accepted. They love criticism. 'Any publicity is good publicity,' I laugh. But Paolo feels this is reductive. 'If we inspire debate we have achieved something.' Debate is another word beyond reproach, it seems, though only certain outcomes are acceptable. Paolo is telling me that Luciano Benetton is way out in front in this regard. He wants to provoke serious reflection on the role of capitalism in contemporary society. He wants to show that you can be successful *and* committed to improving people's lot. I suggest that as a wealthy man, Mr Benetton could well donate a tithe to the poor without drawing attention to his largesse. To annoy him I quote: 'Take heed that ye do not your alms before men, to be seen of them. . .' 'In that case nothing would ever be done,' Paolo comes back. For the first time it occurs to me that this practising Catholic is more pessimistic than I. I do believe there are people who give unobtrusively. Though when I learned all those Bible verses I quote it was to have golden stars stuck beside my name at Sunday School.

The plane lands in Palermo. The people whose lot we are setting out to improve are the Corleonesi. As luck would have it, they are not suffering from the effects of a toxic cloud released by an uncaring multinational, nor are they victims of genocide, famine, drought, civil war or the AIDS epidemic. Rather, their notoriety as a Mafia town has ruined their economy: no one will invest, no one will take them seriously, no one will visit. Above all, they are all to a man vilified as corrupt. Complete pariahs. Now, however, there is a new mayor who has been voted in on an anti-Mafia ticket. He and his staff have launched a campaign to change the image of the town and attract investment. Their masterstroke, in terms of press coverage, was to phone Benetton and invite them to get involved. In an interview, the famous Benetton photographer Oliviero Toscani has already suggested that the people of Corleone should bring a libel action against Mario Puzo for having ruined the town's reputation for ever. He himself now regrets, Toscani says, that one of those powerful images with which Benetton likes to shock the public showed a Mafia victim sprawled in blood. . .

That most incitement to charity is based on an appeal to guilt seems obvious enough. The crucifixion story establishes once and for all that our contemplation of pathos is to be accompanied by a recognition that we are party to the crime. The Son of Man died for *our* sins. In Judas we betrayed him. In Peter we denied him. In Pilate we washed our hands of him. *Mea culpa, mea maxima culpa.* Thus when I see people slaughtered in Rwanda, I know it is a legacy of Western imperialism. When I see legless children in Bosnian hospitals I know it is because we didn't care as much about Sarajevo as about the oilfields of Kuwait. When I see homeless young people on the streets of my town it can only be because I voted for an uncaring government. But what exactly is the nature of the guilt I must assuage with respect to the people of Corleone?

The town sizzles in dusty heat on a low hillside. In narrow streets the heavy traffic is at once hectic and static. Immediately, the eye spots the name of an infamous Mafia boss, Riina. Rather than in newspaper headlines, it appears here on a shop-front ominously announcing: FRESH MEATS – FROM RIINA & BROS. As if to compensate, the main square is Piazza Falcone & Borsellino, two magistrates for whose murder Riina has been held responsible. Our hotel is a modern construction on the hill above the town beside a large restaurant and reception centre built by the same proprietors. Locals occasionally express doubt as to where all that money came from. Driving here to the campaign's first press conference, its local organizer, Raffaele Turtula, offered a lift to two young figures in the gathering gloom.

103

French. They had come to sniff the air in Mafia-town. *Où se trouve la maison de Totò Riina?* I myself was to attend a press conference given by the youth of the town on the afternoon of my arrival. When a journalist asked, were schoolchildren aware of a difference between those from Mafia families and the others, two or three shrill voices protested: 'Oh but why do you always have to speak of the Mafia? You think of nothing but Mafia when you come to Corleone!' And I realize that we are guilty, quite simply, of having thought ill of these people. Carelessly, we have not remembered to distinguish between the malignant individual (or organization) and the benign community. Of Man.

In his book *The Ruin of Kasch*, Roberto Calasso has some provocative pages on that hero of democracies, La Fayette, the Frenchman's flair for striking fine attitudes in his pursuit of popularity. Calasso remarks: 'With La Fayette the alliance between Good Causes and Stupidity is signed and sealed. From now on, those who seek the good of Mankind will share a crude, imprecise, warm-hearted, obtuse, emphatic vision of men.' Clearly the whole post-Christian enterprise of substituting God with Man becomes problematic if we forget to have as high an opinion of the latter as we once entertained of the former.

In the event, it is not difficult to like the people of Corleone. At least the ones the Benetton press office can introduce you to. Or Oliviero Toscani for that matter. He's a big, bearded fellow with a ready laugh and pleasant manner. 'People are wonderful, but democracy stinks,' he growls apropos of I can't remember what. He's in the town's pretty public gardens – palm trees and porphyry paths – preparing some adolescents to have their photos taken. In Benetton garments. Cunningly, the company is combining its sponsorship of the mayor's promotional campaign with a Corleone edition of *Colors* and a new Benetton catalogue. They have decided that they will only feature young people in Corleone, this to combat the prevailing image of an ageing, obtuse, inward-looking society. The team's wry French hairdresser remarks on the 'jolie transparence' of one girl's blouse. On a mobile phone, a secretary has taken a call from another local girl who is cancelling. She doesn't want to come. The secretary tries to persuade her. In the background, she tells me later, a father's voice was shouting: 'I'm not having you going there to play the whore!' While journalists mill and would-be models pose, a group of elderly men look on from a line of stone benches. They do not bring their womenfolk when they walk out. Their suits are formal, their faces expressionless.

A goat's severed head has been placed on the doorstep of the mayor's delightful fiancée. 'Typical gesture of local folklore,' he remarks with enviable sang-froid. His name is Pippo Cipriani. He is very young, hook-nosed, has the eager solemnity of a Mormon. At least he and Turtula do not try to play down the Mafia. The organization is in retreat after recent arrests, unable to influence public contracts in the present climate. But they'll be back. Hence the importance of opening up the town fast, giving people the impression that normality is possible. I ask them why they are so obsessed by the image aspect. In short, why do they want the likes of me around? What can it possibly matter what people think about Corleone in London and New York? Very little, they admit. But it matters enormously that the locals see that the world is thinking about them differently. It will help them to believe in change. I warm to these two men. They seem attractive and genuine, happy to attach their careers to a project that will make life easier and safer for their voters. So I'm taken aback when, at the end of a press conference, Paolo stands up and delivers a speech likening Benetton's commitment around the world to that of the new town council in Corleone. Cipriani and company, I reflect, risk seriously unpleasant reprisals. Perhaps even assassination. Benetton, nothing at all. When I mention this to the mayor's brother he says, 'We're normal enough to be exploited, like anybody else.'

Sicilian hospitality is suffocating. The proprietor of a restaurant just will not understand that we do not want everything on his menu. Perhaps he would like the journalists present to recommend his restaurant in their articles. Everybody is given a business card. Paolo is saying that the truth of an image does not reside in any factual element – whether the clothes from Bosnia were really clothes from Bosnia, or the lumps of meat really human hearts – but in the image's capacity to move one to the good, its impact. As with the unspecified 'commitment', there is the assumption that the nature of 'the good' is beyond discussion, that any Benetton impact will be the right impact. Also there is the disturbing acceptance that shocking images, hitherto the preserve of journalism and fiction, are now to emerge as oddly detached forms of persuasion, sanctioned neither by their authenticity, nor their part in a larger narrative. Where will it end? Will we one day be exposed to scenes of appalling cruelty on distant planets, Martian's unmartianity to Martian? Will we be exhorted to save the universe? Madder still, but more endearing, Olivieri is saying, apropos of his third wife's children, that baptism is a form of paedophilia. Master of the provocative *non sequitur*, one suspects he lacks the clarity that might allow for serious reflection. The Sicilian proprietor brings ice-creams that nobody ordered. Then at the till this jolly man offers to issue a receipt rather higher than the real tab, 'if that will help with expense claims,' he says. 'And we came here to improve their image,' somebody mutters.

For all its rejection of salvation by works, it is implicit in the Bible that one performs charity as part of a project to save oneself. 'Master, what good thing shall I do that I may have eternal life?' 'Go and sell that thou hast and give to the poor.' Even Paul's warning that 'without charity' a generous gesture 'profiteth me nothing' suggests that a properly charitable disposition will bring a return of some variety, presumably beyond the grave. But surely few of those who insist on charitable works today, or on inciting others to charitable works, or on cleaning up the Mafia for that matter, actually believe in a Christian paradise. Or am I wrong? Are people still trying to conquer the sky? Even if they'd rather not say so. The Romanian philosopher, Emil

Cioran, had a different understanding of the psychology of
it. When we seek to help, heal or convert others, he wrote,
we are merely eager for them to suffer in the special way we
do. Does that sound bizarre, inexplicable? Leaving Corleone before the rest of the group, Paolo gives me a book he
has written, an analysis of the state of the media in the
modern world. It turns out to be a compendium of
quotations and descriptions aimed at showing how utterly
decadent, violent and valueless society has become. I would
quote from it here, had I not, with a vague fear of
contamination, chosen to leave the thing, like a Gideons'
bible, in my hotel room. It occurs to me that the two
explanations of charity are not mutually exclusive. The
suffering one wishes others to share is precisely this anxious
vision of a world so awful it requires our immediate
intervention, in order to save. . .ourselves. No one must
relax and enjoy what they have.

Not even children. On my return to Verona I find a heap
of scrawled letters on my desk. My daughter's class have
been invited to express their opinions on peace, love and
war. These are now to be sent to the Secretary-General of
the United Nations. But first they must be translated into
English. The teacher, who has recently been given an award
in recognition of her 'humanitarian initiatives', has attached
a polite request: she knows how deeply committed I am,
but could I help with this consciousness-raising project?
Then as I set about deciphering the childish handwriting, I
burst out laughing. I am reminded of a jet-lagged breakfast
in Australia. It was a literary festival and the Pulitzer winner,

Barry Lopez, happened to be sitting next to me. The world was changing for the good, he said, and we must write to encourage that change. This across a sumptuous table at the Adelaide Hilton. 'I think peace is people loving each other,' I translate, 'and being happy not sad and shooting guns.' Perhaps I'm doing what Barry wanted at last.

Is it really incumbent on me to help people? Any people. Does my writing, which I see as the huge pleasure of getting a mental fix on the world, have to be an arrow aimed in a particular and pious direction? Corleone, Rwanda. Suffering faces float up on the screen. Images of torture, of famine, of death. How well TV mediates between the concrete world of those people we can touch and talk to and the safer abstract of mankind! These refugee Rwandans are real people – we know that – but they never smell or beg or answer back. What excellent neighbours! A number flashes on and off. A code. And now somebody is tapping it out, announcing other numbers in a monotone. This much, that much. Dollars, lire, pounds. People are giving. Names, addresses. Then a shiver of release, as after other compulsive acts. Implacable opponent of any form of altruism, Max Stirner wrote in 1844: 'You think disinterestedness does not exist then! On the contrary, nothing is more common! One might even define it as a fashion accessory in the civilized world.' And he explains, 'Disinterestedness begins with the identification of something outside of ourselves which is sacred: mankind.' We bow down before it and become its slaves. Reflecting that I must be careful in my article on Corleone not to introduce any details (the restaurant scene particularly) which might suggest, in the Italian press, a prejudice against the South, I am suddenly aware of entering the realm of the politically correct. And what is political correctness if not enslavement to the universal sacredness of man-(and woman)-kind, our constant apprehension of the offence that might be generated by a careless, or honest, word. But no doubt it was always very difficult to tell the truth.

'Because thou art lukewarm, and neither cold nor hot I will spue thee out of my mouth.' If Paul's verse on charity was one of the most perplexing for a child, then this from the Book of Revelation was perhaps the most frightening. Christianity has a way of presenting us with a radical either–or, as its pious descendants can still choose to spew you out of their mouths if you are not eager to say the right things about Rwanda. For myself, I always knew I was neither cold nor hot. I respond badly to the commandment to love people indiscriminately. Any good I may do will always be incidental to my main path in life. Yet I feel there must be a space between the malignance and cruelty of, say, the Mafia – or even just indifference, meanness, ungenerosity – and this business of being constantly, obsessively concerned that it is our duty to set all wrongs to right. Perhaps the key lies in not seeking to be saved, in not wanting to be seen to be good. So I'll say quite clearly that my article on Corleone, eventually prepared for the newspaper *La Repubblica*, was written for money, with no sense of contributing to change in the world, and if it was positive, as they say, about developments in the Sicilian town, that was because I met Cipriani and Turtula and liked them and got the impression that they could be trusted. As one is willing to help somebody one likes who crosses one's path.

Come Christmas, a box arrived. And though I remember having made it very clear that this was not something I wanted, I found myself unwrapping a Benetton pullover. Then, perhaps Christmas Day itself, moved to tears by some snatch of music, or maybe it was the story of the two-year-old drowned in a nearby fishpond, I grabbed my own youngest child in my arms. 'Lucia!' I kissed her. She slipped and pulled at the collar of my fashionable new sweater. 'Papà!' A hole appeared where the seams meet. Well, I'm not saying that this garment is poor quality, but I have purchased things in discount basements that have survived all three children. Not to mention the woollens my wife put so much love into. In the interests of humankind, perhaps this is a problem to which Luciano Benetton might reasonably devote some attention.

Magic

A great deal has to happen before one person can usefully give advice to another, writes Rilke in his *Letters to a Young Poet*. Across the open plan of the English Language faculty room, I can hear two colleagues discussing the marking procedure for students' examination essays. Apparently this involves deciding what constitutes an error and how the errors are to be counted: in half- or quarter-marks subtracted from an ideal total of thirty. In my own cubicle I am, as usual, trying to do too much. To one side I have a heap of photo-books which I am supposed to be reviewing. Occasionally I glance over at them, turning a page or two, while officially getting on with reading my students' theses. A man on a camel is speaking into a mobile phone. A newborn's crib is plastered with photographs of ageing rabbis. 'Written in the 1940s, the work examines the changing condition of women in a patriarchal society before and during the Second War,' writes one student of Christina Stead's *Letty Fox, Her Luck*. Would I ever want to read a novel described thus? But the text of Rick Smolan's *Passage to Vietnam* is hardly more inspiring. Beside a powerful image of a young woman leaning into the oars of her sampan, the caption remarks: 'The Mekong is two thousand miles long and splits into nine separate channels before emptying into the South China Sea.' Well, well.

But now my colleagues have started arguing. One student is found to have scored minus five. 'She is very intelligent, though. I know her.' The girl has made seventy mistakes. There is some discussion as to whether these are not mostly the same mistake, since she used the wrong tense throughout. What she has written is interesting. But how can that ever be quantified? Or indeed the affection that the teacher objecting clearly has for the girl. 'The shift from a shocking presentation of sexual perversion to an interest in society's approach to child education shows a growing maturity,' writes another student of Ian McEwan. My eye strays to an image of a Bombay prostitute giggling behind her hand in a shack. Maturity. What a wealth of condescension in the word! But my first student has arrived. Miss *Mrs Dalloway*.

The faculty room is rigidly laid out. Our university has a bright new building on the industrial outskirts of Milan. There are rows of cubicles – lozenges of some mauve fabric on screens of grey and glass – then the remorseless rectangles of floor tiles, windows, desks, cabinets, ceiling grilles. Sometimes I wonder if this environment doesn't encourage a digital and pedantic approach to learning assessment. As indeed the whole modern world tends to suggest that what is in line cannot be wrong, an ethos enshrined in the collocation 'right angle'. Amusingly, though, the right-minded designers of our *palazzo* did not think of the practicalities of tutorials. Caught in a cubicle, there is nowhere for this young woman to sit, except right next to me, inches away. The moment she crosses her long legs, leans forward with her papers and perfume, an

113

intimacy is generated, an awareness of man and woman that while it might be the subject of many of the books we discuss is rarely broached in the faculty room. In *Villas of Tuscany*, I observed a few minutes ago, fig leaves had been carefully distributed across a sylvan scene of nymphs and satyrs.

Right-angled, right-minded. Could it be that there is a sort of pact between conventional morality and the information culture? At the expense of deeper knowledge? Is it the same pact that fixed the fig leaf? My student's thesis, like so many others, offers useful information about the author, the the background, side by side with praise of the author's commitment to liberal values. Occasionally these two strands twine together, in remarks like: 'the author lived in an age when women writers were at a disadvantage', but there is never any useful traffic between them, no pertinent engagement with the text, or indeed with anything. I suggest to this young woman that she hasn't begun to explain why *Mrs Dalloway* is enjoyable, or convincing – if it is – or even what its real content might be. She asks me if she will be able to graduate this session. Every Italian student has to complete a thesis to get a degree. For many the accumulation of two hundred or so written pages is as near to torture as the education system will bring them. Looking at her dressy clothes and rings, I decide that she probably is not worried about another semester's fees. 'The thesis could be much improved,' I remark. Her eyes plead. Unprofessionally, I say: 'Tell me your problem.' 'I have to get married,' she says. I point out that a degree is not a prerequisite for holy wedlock. The eyes plead harder.

Definitely out of line now, I ask: 'Your fiancé refuses to marry you unless you already have your degree?' She shakes her head. 'You were planning to move away and if you don't graduate you won't be able to?' Again she shakes her head. Then, having lived in Italy nearly twenty years now, I get it at the third. 'Your fiancé's *mother* doesn't want him to marry someone who doesn't have a degree?' She stares. How did I guess? I add: 'And he wouldn't dream of upsetting her, of course.' She nods, unhappy and embarrassed, but trying to laugh. The man is thirty-two. 'It's a miracle I got him to agree to leave home at all. He's so attached to his mother.' Who better, I wonder, than this young student to offer me some perceptive reflections on Clarissa Dalloway's fears of invasiveness, Woolf's obsession with territory and the nature of the claims we have on each other. 'Tell your *fidanzato*,' I suggest, 'that your tutor feels you are far too good to finish in a hurry.'

There. I have influenced someone's life. Officially, of course, I was merely taking a decision on the adequacy or otherwise of an anonymous thesis. I'm aware that compartmentalization and impersonality are hard-won virtues without which civilization would be difficult indeed. But what do I really care about the quality of a thesis? I've let worse ones through. No, my decision was at least partly prompted by the entirely inappropriate reflection that if this young woman doesn't deal with her fiancé's mother now, it may be even more difficult later on. Why do I get involved like this? Why can't I draw a line?

I turn back to the photo-books. Frescoed horses seem to

115

explode from a cinquecento ceiling for the rape of young Persephone. In the Rajput fort at Kota, princess and maharaja ride after a great black boar in the centre of a mural that whirls with boats and elephants and wrestlers and dancers. If one were teaching mathematics, I reflect, examining an attractive Vietnamese woman writing equations on a blackboard, there would be no problem. The subject itself is the epitome of abstraction, a play of digital equivalences whose referents need not concern us, its acquisition pure mental power that can be harnessed as convention dictates: calculate this, calculate that; build a bridge, blow it up. But how can the knowledge I am eager for my students to achieve be compartmentalized when its referents are everything we most intimately feel? And how or in what direction harnessed, if it is a knowledge that breaks down pieties, revels in perplexities? Perhaps the boyfriend will delay the ceremony. Pride hurt, she leaves him. Turns anorexic? When they might have been perfectly happy! The book on Pakistan, I recall, had a photo of an ecstatic young country bride at what was doubtless an arranged marriage.

My colleagues have agreed to mark all the errors first before deciding whether they count as a loss of a quarter-mark or a half-mark and whether similar errors are to count once or more than once. In this way a certain amount of control can be achieved over the way the results are presented. In extreme cases the quality of the content can be used as an excuse to explain the addition or subtraction of a few points. A certain homogeneity is essential. Meantime, I am becoming obsessed by the distance between text and image in these photo-books: the one so dull and plodding – and full of numbers; the other so powerful and rich – and evidently beyond the realm of any counting and measuring. It is as if the publishers were seeking to alleviate a presumed uneasiness on the part of the reader. They want to reassure us that we have not wasted our money on a mere collection of photographs, are not simply satisfying escapist fantasies. No, we are accumulating information. A woman sits on a buffalo under pouring rain, precariously beautiful against a landscape of paddy-fields and telegraph poles. 'Rural electrification projects have a long way to go,' the text remarks.

Information, formulas, morals: just as our own prejudices are never more embarrassingly naked than when heard from the mouths of our infant children, so society's bolt-holes are pitifully exposed in the theses of my students. 'Knowledge is above all the comedy of knowledge.' Thus Nietzsche. And, 'No, I'm not really interested,' I tell my next student, 'in the exact date of the newspaper in which this or that interview was published.' It's Miss Letty Fox, the thesis on Christina Stead. All my students but one are women. This too is in the scheme of things and again has to do with the way all learning must be harnessed to some end or another. The men are to be executives and engineers: they don't need or want to know about literature. The women are to be teachers and multilingual secretaries. This is perfectly understandable: a body of data strains between the shafts while received wisdom wields the whip. Still, there is something wondrous about the way so many of these women's theses speak of feminist achievements, when the university we work in is segregated with almost Islamic severity.

Then I am just saying that one can hardly choose to

117

praise an author for her politics or feel one has accounted for Stead's novels by identifying their autobiographical content, when something occurs to me. A scholarly article I read somewhere, about Ovid and the gap between written commentaries and pictorial illustrations of his *Metamorphoses*. The scholars debunk the myths, this interesting though rather difficult article said, explain them away in scientific and sociological systems, while paintings and sculptures endorse and exalt them, keep their ancient intuitions alive and potent. But only in the grotto, or ghetto of art. And what I would like to jot down – but I can't, because I'm listening to the student telling me that Stead herself, like Letty, was a member of the Socialist Party – is that perhaps this is the same gulf that opens up in these photo-books. Bland information, authoritatively delivered on the one hand. Talk of history and progress. And then these images that actually speak to us with a directness beyond anything in the text: a particular way men and women have of being together (on a street in Jerusalem), an intimate sense of our place in the landscape (on the shores of the Dead Sea). Suddenly I'm quite excited by this idea and interrupt the girl to say: 'The problem is that there's an enormous gap between the vitality of this novel and the sort of things you are writing about it. The real achievement would be to say something interesting about the magic of the thing.' Remarkably, the girl looks me straight in the eyes and says: 'I know. But how?'

Over a lunch of toasted sandwich and Coca-Cola a colleague objects that we must not make value judgements, because they can never be properly verified. She writes challenging deconstructionist analyses for small university reviews. The canteen presents a pitched battle between the right-angled inspirations of architect and authorities and the appetites and instincts of the students. Smoking is forbidden but indulged in at doorways. The tables are littered with paper plates and plastic cups, the chairs dragged here and there among bags and coats. Voices clatter. 'Perhaps it's a question of complexity,' I suggest. 'One admires those books whose complexity of content and vision gets closest to the grain of our experience.' And immediately I wish I'd said this to my student. So I add: 'Isn't it a little like the whole question of election in the end? I mean, with some students you just know that they are among the elect. It's an intuition you can't avoid. They understand, even if they haven't yet learned how to articulate. Whereas with others, however hard you try, you feel they never will.' She objects that this is pure elitism. 'The Indians,' I tell her, 'believed that some people were born with a portion of a god in them. And others not. They called it *amsa*.' But this actually makes her angry. Next I'll be wanting to introduce a caste system. To avoid conflict, we change the subject: cinema chat; Woody Allen, whom she likes a great deal; Hugh Grant. And did I know, she suddenly interrupts herself, that a close friend of ours was propositioned at that recent conference, 'Literature and the Internet'? By a married man! Isn't that appalling? On the mere excuse that there had been some mistake with the bookings and they had to share a room. I grin. 'But you wouldn't do that, would you?' she demands. While it seems one cannot talk about the magic of a book, it is apparently extremely easy to say how people should behave. I wonder who will have the courage to tell her that her hair is very beautiful.

Wittgenstein remarked: '*that* the world exists is far more amazing than any *how* the world exists'. And back in my cubicle I decide the best of the photo-books that I have to review is the one that has no text: *Bombay*, by Raghubir Singh. Men in coloured shorts with sacks of cement on their heads. A fat cross-legged sitar player with a purple shirt. Shoulders heaving a cart through heavy traffic. Each image vibrates with a life that comes together for just that fraction of a second the shutter clicks: street scenes broken up by reflecting surfaces, a shop window, a mirror, slum dwellings scissored by a shaft of sunlight. Everything is complicated, but awesomely obvious. And everywhere faces: glum, smiling, animated, reticent. Bright eyes gleam out of poverty or wealth. There is a perilous luminous presence here that goes far beyond any social comment.

The phone rings. It's a student from far-away Cagliari wanting to know how many points she can expect for her thesis. The system is complicated. Her average is only ninety-five, but it should be remembered that she has done three languages, thus three fourth-year written exams, which tend to bring the average down. Will the Commission compensate by giving more points for the thesis? If she graduates with more than a hundred there is a scholarship she can apply for. 'How long does the summary in English have to be?' She is nervous. A man is shouting something in the background. Her father perhaps. 'About 10 per cent of overall length,' I find myself replying. And I do so automatically, easily. For if it is true that our civilization is going through a vast and arduous process of unlearning, of exclusion, forgetting even, what we get in return is the exhilaration of efficiency, the gratifying impression of getting things done. Theses, for example. 'To be left on my desk at least two weeks before final submission,' I tell her with great authority.

Back from their lunch, grappling with those notorious written exams, my colleagues in the next cubicle are trying to decide whether use of the pluperfect is essential to indicate an action prior to the narrative tense. Can one write, 'He said she went home early'? Or must it be, 'had gone home early'? A little late myself, I get up to go to teach. But stop at their cubicle. 'In Ireland they say, "He had said she went home early." We laugh together, because everybody knows how crazy it is to pin these things down. Yet people do make mistakes.

I labour under a superstition that the more sophisticated the means of communication, the more superficial the content communicated. Perhaps this comes as a result of watching TV. Or reading the speeches in Thucydides. In any event I don't turn on the classroom microphone. Or the overhead video. In the end I only have twenty students and the problem is not to be heard but to find some way of articulating what I think I know. Or know I don't. I invite a student to turn off her mobile phone. Two or three position their cassette recorders. We are considering the relationship of various novels to the language they were written in. What happens when you translate them? I give examples, encouraging the students to savour the different focusing of English and Italian sentence structures. I have anecdotes, rules of thumb, comments on the resources and culture of each linguistic tradition. For they must have something to write down. But behind it all, I know, is some material as elusive and numinous as life itself. Far from equivalences or principles, one is groping for the place where the word adheres to the mind, for the way the mind represents itelf to itself, through the word, through the world. Beyond the students' heads a wall of windows opens on derelict factories, steaming power-stacks. The winter sky is already trailing its colours. At 4.30 sharp a goods train will drown out my voice, clanking through an encampment of gypsies. Suddenly I'm aware of twenty pairs of eyes communicating puzzled smiles. Apparently I have left a rather longer pause than usual.

There are positive and negative ways of looking at this, of course, depending, I suppose, on whether one is desperate for answers, or has learned to love the questions. Once, at a moment of some crisis in my life, when I was more or less the same age as the girls sitting in front of me, I scribbled: 'Consider the irony of having a mind that once believed itself big enough to get round everything. But it isn't. Again and again it retreats into bewilderment. Until bewilderment is what it chiefly knows. What it knows are repeated approaches, some meticulous, some ingenious, all in vain, to the fog of bewilderment.' But on brighter days, and especially past a certain point in life, one might want to call that bewilderment magic, or as Raghubir Singh would probably say, *maya*. 'That was my pause for the goods train,' I tell the students. 'Just got the timing wrong.'

Returning to the faculty room, I prepare for the arrival of my last student. She is my brightest and I have high hopes for her. Through a comparison of the Italian translation of *Women in Love* and the original, she is trying to put her finger on what the book is really about and the way it generates the emotions it does. Repeatedly she appears upset by things she has discovered about Lawrence's life: outrageous things he said, mainly, at the expense of women. She hadn't expected that of a great writer. But her mind is lucid and engaged, her analyses to the point. Her perfume invades my cubicle. Perhaps I can discuss with her what I have been thinking about? In relation, perhaps, to Lawrence's insistence on the continuity between corruption and vitality, his obsessive use of antithetical collocation. She sits down, inches away. 'Right, about this question of the biblical language in the chapter "The Excurse".' But my student stops me. She puts a soft hand on my arm. She has decided not to complete her thesis. She has been offered a job in London, and though it is not a good job, she is going to take it. She wants to leave home.

The exact words Rilke wrote, or at least in their English translation, go as follows: 'for ultimately, and precisely in the deepest and most important matters, we are unspeakably alone; and many things must go right, a whole constellation of events must be fulfilled, for one human being successfully to advise or help another'. And perhaps this conclusion is no more than the obvious consequence of the German poet's other remark that 'things are not all so tangible and sayable as people would usually have us believe'. Anyhow, day over, I head for the station. Here there's the business of checking the timetable. Is the 6.15 weekends only? Is it a *rapido* or an *inter-regionale*? Do I need a supplement? First class or second? Platform number? Don't forget to stamp your ticket! It's complicated, but one soon learns the ropes – the corridors, the escalators – whereas my student resisted all attempts to persuade her she was making a mistake. The train slides knowingly through a great maze of rails – as the practised mind through equations, through rules and regulations, tangles of grammar, the labyrinth of the Internet. One is right to be proud of efficiency, of course, but it is the enigma that calls to us. Using words I suspect were borrowed from Lawrence, she said, 'I've felt this growing inside me for a long time.' Unsettled, I pull out the photo-books. A marble nymph gestures seductively amid sumptuous baroque. Fishermen strut on stilts in the surf off Nam Ha. To the left through my reflected face strings of lights rise through a winter landscape towards the Alps. Only what is impervious to our scheming offers the mind the bewilderment it seeks, the repose in wonder. Despite all the right angles, a young woman's crazy decision can still make you feel the magic of everything that is, our real and incommensurable habitat. Upon which Awakening I fall suddenly asleep.

Destiny

There are those who still believe this word has meaning. One such is an old man who at seventy-plus decided he wasn't through with fighting his wife. What I want to know is what was going on in his head the moment he came down the stairs and with tears in his eyes announced to his son-in-law: 'This is my destiny.'

It is impossible to cram a life into the longest book, never mind a few pages. All the same, the dramatic scene in question may be prefaced by another. The son-in-law – let's call him Frank – is on the phone to his wife's brother, Angelo, son of the old man, whom we can refer to from now on as Babbo, Italian term for Dad. The two young men, Frank and Angelo, one American one Italian, are talking about the fact that the old folks want to divorce. Or say they do. Angelo's mother, Mamma, has demanded all the property, half Babbo's pension, plus whatever it costs to maintain their schizophrenic son, the eldest, now languishing in some closed community. On the phone, Angelo says he washes his hands of his parents. He refuses to see them. Or even talk to them. Babbo has always been a disgrace, he says, going after other women and letting Mamma know. He deserves everything that's coming to him. Frank points out that Mamma is a notoriously difficult woman to get on with: charming and irascible, ever quick to accuse and castigate, usually with slammed doors and sullen silences. 'She does have that hotel receipt,' Angelo remarks, referring to the affair Babbo is recently supposed to have had with an upstairs tenant, an unprepossessing creature of fortyish. 'Look,' Frank says, exchanging glances with his wife, Marta, the only daughter, who is standing at the open kitchen door, 'nobody is denying that Babbo has behaved badly, that he's screwed around, but he put you all through school and did everything for Stefano' – meaning the schizo-phrenic – 'I can't see why you can't give him, or better still your mother, a bed for a night or two, because we can't handle having both of them here. Not at the same time.' Then when the phone is put down, to the immense surprise of both Frank and Marta, Babbo walks downstairs from where he has been listening on the landing. The younger couple had thought he was out picking up their little children from school. 'Thank you for defending me,' Babbo smiles, 'but please note that whatever stories may be told about me, I have never "screwed around", as you put it.' He seems immensely pleased with this dignified perform-ance, so different from the shaken, tearful figure who will descend the same stairs the following afternoon.

In any event, you are beginning to get the picture. A life suppurating with unpleasant incident. A family where bygones are never bygones. Grudges, hatchets, corpses, are only buried the better to be dug up again. Decay seething with vitality. Babbo says he'll pop out to a hotel before Mamma arrives, as he did last time. Then for a few minutes he speaks ill of her, as she no doubt will of him when she arrives.

The 'last time' – only a few days ago – was when Mamma came up north to visit the schizophrenic Stefano whose community is nearby. It was one of the rare occasions when he had permission to go out, though only if accompanied by both his parents. Since Babbo refused to go with her, she pretended her husband was waiting outside in the car because illegally parked. The community official was not taken in. Both parents must sign out the patient in person. Now Mamma is frantic that she will never be able to spend time with her eldest son if Babbo refuses to cooperate. Just as it took two to procreate the boy – for she still thinks of this obese forty-five-year-old schizophrenic as a boy – it now takes two to have his company. Divorce becomes unfeasible. There is a knot somewhere that won't come undone.

One way of dealing with such Gordian tangles, of course, is to heave a sharpened sword. Thus Alexander claimed vast new territories for his crown, thus countless others have abandoned their chains to explore new marriages, new predicaments: the blade hacks, the coils give, people are free to breathe and regret. Having been locked out of his house some six weeks ago, upon Mamma's discovery of the credit-card bill indicating payment for a double room in a nearby seaside hotel, Babbo claims to have reached this critical point. Since then he has been staying with his daughter Marta and son-in-law Frank. But while it whirls and glitters round his balding head, somehow the great blade never descends to sever the knot, but seems rather to trace further arabesques in the air. The separation is not finalized. Indeed, Marta and Frank have begun to suspect that Babbo is merely trying to make Mamma jealous by monopolizing the grandchildren, particularly the youngest, their delightful two-year-old daughter. Unless the truth is simply that nothing is less likely to lead to change, than talk of change. A destiny is cemented, perhaps, by dreams of happenstance and peripeteia. So Christ at Gethsemane prayed the cup might pass, well aware that this was not His Father's will.

Alternatively, there are those who claim such embroilments can, with patience, be disentangled. Even if only for examination. The experts, the therapists. The very American Frank, for example, disturbed to find the landscape he has married into thus pitted with shallow and decidedly unquiet graves, is attempting to get his bearings by reading a book called *Psychotic Games in the Family* – another metaphor for protracted conflict where exhumations and knotty hitches can now be seen, through an analyst's eye, as move and counter-move in a deadlocked game. This notion puts Frank in mind that he may be able to blow the whistle on it all. 'Don't scuttle off to a hotel when Mamma comes again,' he tells his Italian father-in-law. 'That would be as much a sign of weakness as going away with her just because she came to get you. Then there'll never be an end to this story. Wouldn't it be better if I met her at the door and told her that you don't intend to see her, that you're serious about the divorce, and that she can stay with Angelo until it's sorted out? Then maybe we can reach some solution.' Thus, some hours later, we have the telephone conversation already described, followed by Babbo's majestic, paunch-led descent down suburban stairs with declarations at once of innocence and resolution.

The central thesis of *Psychotic Games in the Family* is that the families of schizophrenic children are characterized by a long-running, never-to-be-resolved antagonism between the parents, each of whom seeks to draw the unfortunate child into a privileged relationship with themselves against their partner. In his or her desire to grow up, the child welcomes this intimacy, only to sense at some later stage that he, or she, has been nothing more than a bargaining chip in the game being played out between father and mother. At which point, with a thousand other factors playing their part, disillusion and resentment may seek their inarticulate outlet in pathology.

Reading this heady material, Frank sees many parallels with what he knows about Marta's family and, perhaps drawn by the idea of the game, as the mind is ever beguiled into creativity by analogy, he thinks of chess. Babbo and Mamma, whom he loves very much, are now long past the complex middle-game gambits that perhaps contributed to Stefano's schizophrenia. It's too late to undo that now, too late to say, If I just took back this or that move, or, If only I had played a different opening . . . No, these old folks are in one of those impossible endgame situations where neither white nor black can ever win, the kings roaming pointlessly across the squares, chasing and repelling each other, but without the power to make a kill. Time, then, to inform them that once the pawns are gone, the rules stipulate no

129

more than fifty moves to stalemate. After which forces must be disengaged, the board closed.

Frank has high hopes.

That Mamma is indeed coming a second time the younger couple know because the old folk's neighbours, three hundred miles away, have phoned to say that, after returning exhausted from her last attempt to visit her sick son, the old lady spent but a couple of days expressing her fury to all and sundry, then set off again. Early this morning. And where to, if not to Stefano and Babbo? Stefano via Babbo, Mamma would say. Though perhaps the truth is more Babbo via Stefano. In any event this initiative on the neighbours' part, their phoning to warn of Mamma's arrival, surprises no one. Every drama attracts – requires – its audience and stage crew. Without the spotlights, without the *schadenfreude* they vouchsafe to others, where would the actors find the energy to go at it with such demonic zeal? Would Hamlet's player have wept, without witnesses, for Hecuba? As Mamma strikes up the garden path, probably well aware she is expected, even observed, she looks exhausted, yes, and dishevelled, but at least she seems to know what she's about, she has rehearsed her part, and this gives her an air, if not of happiness, at least of determination, the grim satisfaction, even in disaster, of knowing who one is, and that others are paying attention. Christ, one feels, might have suffered less had His Father let the cup pass, but who would He have been without His crucifixion? Or Scott had he come back? Or Nelson without his final 'kismet'? And if none can be resurrected in the public mind unless they embrace their destiny, it goes without saying that an attentive audience can create a sense of purpose. Even if it apparently leads to calamity. Mamma will not disappoint.

But Frank is ready. Even before Mamma rings, he opens the front door and greets her as she climbs the condo stairs to their duplex. Gently, he asks her what she is doing, arriving unannounced. Usually she phones. And he suggests, as kindly as he can, that it would be better if she went to stay with Angelo, or in a hotel. Until things have been sorted out with her husband. For Babbo is serious, Frank tells Mamma, about separating. She brushes past him. Without removing her coat, she goes straight to the kitchen, opens the fridge, finds cheese, bread, wine. Perhaps aware she is in need of strength, she eats ravenously, scornfully. 'He's skulking upstairs, I presume?' And Mamma makes it clear she's not leaving without him. Without him she can't see Stefano, her firstborn.

Mamma drinks off two tumblers of wine before Frank can remove the bottle. Marta is out, unfortunately, but he phones Angelo and asks him to come and help. Angelo prevaricates. Nevertheless, Frank feels quite sure of what he is about: these two people, he says to himself, Babbo and Mamma, do nothing but upset each other and those around them. It's time to help them to help themselves. He is experiencing that dangerous and peculiarly modern delirium of he who imagines that a little knowledge and related technique can dissolve decades of antagonism. Perhaps not unlike an American Secretary of State on a peace mission to Palestine.

At this point Frank's two older children come home from school. 'To think,' Mamma is shouting, 'how that bastard would kiss his own kids with his mouth still mucky from the knickers of his rotten sluts.' Frank objects that this is over the top and dispatches the children upstairs to watch television. She must go if she cannot desist from saying such things. She must go anyway, since Babbo has no intention of seeing her. As he says this, Frank is aware that Babbo, no doubt listening from the top of the stairs, will now have to contend with Japanese cartoons in the background: Ken Shiro, the technique of Okutu. 'You'll feel so much better once you've broken off this obsession,' Frank explains to his seventy-year-old mother-in-law, and adds that he's sure that after a little while of healthy separation Babbo will be more than ready to go with her to visit Stefano. Then, since no one in this family has ever really washed their hands of anything, Angelo arrives after all.

Could it be that everything that partakes of life, everything vital, is essentially unbalanced? Is this the scandal that underlies all others? That only the sick are interesting? That only suffering offers potential meaning, while nothing fills the existential void like the fizz of a neurotic mind, the back and forth of an embattled relationship? In any event Angelo tries to make light. 'Relax, Mamma. Come over to my place. We can go out to dinner together.' Mamma begins to rave. She will not leave without Babbo. What a miserable coward he is not to come downstairs to talk to her! Frank fixes her a glass of water with some drops of tranquillizer which she pretends to drink, but in fact pours into the children's goldfish bowl. 'Those whom God hath joined together,' she shrieks, 'let no man put asunder!'

Then Frank raises the stakes. He says that if Mamma will not go willingly, he will throw her out, or even call the police. If nothing else, the book he has been reading has given him a sense of the strength of the forces at play in such situations. But perhaps distracted by the text's thera-peutic vocation, he has overlooked one of the deeper messages: that the parents of schizophrenics, while rarely serene are not necessarily unhappy in their eternal antago-nism. Or at least not unspeakably so. Rather, and quite movingly, these embattled couples seem to need each other, not unlike the quarrelling figures in Beckett's plays who ever announce they have had enough, but never leave. That a third human being may be destroyed by this mechanism is a terrible thing, but it doesn't undo the fact that such partners draw their lifeblood from each other's veins. Mutually succouring vampires, their teeth are snugly set at each other's necks. 'I'll kill myself rather than leave without him,' Mamma screams, and she seizes the breadknife.

But what is Babbo thinking upstairs? For it's his mental processes I am interested in, not Mamma's determined melodrama. She knows what she wants; he hesitates. Or appears to. Presumably he is aware of a variety of possible decisions. Is he gratified, as he listens, by her determination to have him? Does it offer a sense to his life? Or is he appalled? Or both? Is he just waiting to see if she will go before he caves in? Or is he thinking of the woman he had the affair with? If he did. Or of other women as well? Perhaps his life is a garden infested with might-have-beens, the way some amateurs can never decide which of three plants must be taken out so that one can grow properly. Could it be, then, that Frank is wrong? That it is not so much a question of the old man's never having been able to leave his wife, as of his never being able serenely, finally, to choose her? Or to feel – for this is another alternative – that he has no choice.

Babbo scratches at a freckled baldness, turns to the TV screen where an expert in obscure martial arts is saving at least the world, perhaps the universe. The children gape. If living means being in thrall to the enchantment of the possible – 'where there's life, there's hope' – then a sense of destiny will presumably involve surrender to the only possible, an acceptance of mortality: this is my one life, my one adventure, the one woman between myself and death. But should we be obliged to *choose* our destiny, rather than merely grasping a sense of it after all is settled? Or rather, if we choose it, was it really destiny? Or just a mistake? Boswell quotes Samuel Johnson as remarking that the overall sum of human weal and woe would not be greatly altered if marriages were imposed by the public registrar. And our immediate thought on reading those words is that Johnson is trying to tell us that random selection is as good, and bad, as pondered choice when it comes to the pairing of men and women, that one cannot know with whom one will be happy, or indeed with whom one might have had a profitable unhappiness. But looked at another way, perhaps what Johnson meant was that if only our partner had been imposed, had been perceived as fate rather than choice, we would not fret so. The way few fret because they were born male, or female, or found themselves growing up in Asia, or in Edinburgh. One's partner would be accepted as part of the landscape, something to come to terms with: in fine weather congenial; dismal in the thin rain of November; under storm clouds menacing. Downstairs there is a loud shriek and the sound of a scuffle.

Then how is it – and Babbo once shared this thought with Frank, with whom he has often sought complicity against Mamma in the couple's age-old game of seducing third parties in order to hurt and keep each other – how is it that having chosen something, it may come, over the years, to seem imposed upon us, like the most terrible edict from the highest authority? So that one has both the responsibility of the choice and the impotence of the victim. This is discouraging, but might at least have led to resignation, had not the can of worms been opened again by the possibility of divorce. All recent development – social development – in the West has been worthily directed toward 'increasing individual choice', giving us 'control over our lives', reducing the incidence of imposed destiny. And yet . . . 'Do not offer a three-year-old a choice of diet,' says the child psychology book I have been reading, 'the burden of deciding is too much for him.' But at what age is it not too much? Contraception, abortion, euthanasia – the Pope for one knows we are not ready for them, as we were never really ready, perhaps, to have the sacred texts in our native tongue. Then if we have to decide things for ourselves, or illude ourselves that that's the way things work, then who shall we blame when things go wrong? True, psychoanalysis has offered us the excuse of parent-induced complexes: I continue to make awful choices in life because I was brought up by these monsters (young Angelo makes ample use of this expedient when his various relationships fail). But it is a poor and tortuous determinism to substitute for, say, the edict of an oracle: the boy will kill his father, marry his mother; or for a caste system that allows you to claim: I am here, like it or not, because I was born to this; I am beside this woman, like it or not, because, under the direction of our household gods, our families chose each for the other. The more shape is imposed, the freer I am in my mind to reflect upon it. That said, one would not wish to be walled in a cell.

Downstairs Mamma is screaming. She has turned the knife not on herself, but on Frank, who had picked up the phone, though more as a bluff than because he has really decided to call the police. Angelo, reassured to find his own considerable personal problems once more explained by the madness of his parents, is trying to wrest the weapon from her. Meanwhile, upstairs, while the children watch their cartoon, Babbo still paces back and forth, mulling over and over an ancient stalemate. He was brought up in the twenties and thirties. There was no divorce in Italy then, nor any real prospect of economic ease. Wartime soldiering imposed on him that relief in submission to destiny which no doubt explains why men and women will risk their lives for causes whose outcomes can hardly be of great personal interest to them. Perhaps his happiest period was in an American POW camp, studying English, building military airports. After which, the general rush to marry old girlfriends.

Now, quite suddenly, the child-rearing over, even the necessity to earn over, he finds himself in a world where everything can be renegotiated, where people are learning to live in a constant delirium of choice and possibility. And Frank, his son-in-law, whom he respects, has insisted that it is merely a matter of holding firm. He can have what he wants, what he sometimes imagines he wants: his slippered independence in a quiet little flat somewhere. Away from her. It's just that now the crisis is upon him, the final decision, he finds himself paralysed. Not quite convinced by either the old world or the new, he has the worst of both: the sense, that is, that it would be possible to rearrange his life, if only he were someone else. For the destiny of being oneself, ultimate and unavoidable imposition, is never more humiliatingly evident than when all other constraints are stripped away. A cry and the sound of a body falling start his feet walking down the stairs.

First his shoes appear, then his baggy trousers, tightening toward the paunch. Does he hope that something awful has happened that will decide matters for him? A catastrophe? Now his sweat-stained shirt is in view, now his heaving chest. Does his descent represent a collapse of resolution, a defeat, the inability to imagine another self? Or a triumph of responsible decision: I choose this life, this woman, whatever the drawbacks may be? Did he ever really mean anything more in all this melodrama than to make her see she needed him? By hurting her? To push things to the limit? Whatever the truth, his face, when it comes into view, appears to be melting: his eyes are melting, even the skin seems to be melting from jowls and neck. Frank who has just helped the now dis-armed Mamma to her feet, is appalled. He genuinely wanted to help his father-in-law, but the experience seems to have reduced Babbo to some kind of ghoulish jelly. 'You can't give in now,' Frank protests. His Italian is accented with American. 'It's blackmail. She throws a tantrum and you do what she says.' Babbo cannot look the younger man in the eye. He is moving slowly and deliberately, as though in a trance. 'This is my destiny,' he announces. And repeats, 'My destiny.'

The parents of my own sister-in-law, in the USA, married, divorced, remarried, then divorced again. One reads more and more often of this kind of thing. The mind is liquid, fickle. Who is not familiar with its fast swinging tides, its sudden kaleidoscopic rearrangements of the past? Speaking of beliefs, causes, commitments, the ferocious Max Stirner was quick to scorn people for wanting nothing better than something they could enslave themselves to – religion, love, patriotism – for not having the courage, that is, to check at every turn of the road that their lives were exactly what they wanted. And indeed it may well be that secretly we seek nothing more of marriage – or work, or the city where we live – than to be securely locked away there, as many, entering some extravagant new supermarket, will close their minds and trust to old brand loyalties. On the other hand, who can deny that there must have been a certain serenity in a society that worshipped its ancestors and imposed what it imagined was best on its children? Alone in his living room – Babbo, Mamma and Angelo having gone now, even laughing together surprisingly on the stairs – the disillusioned Frank is left behind in his contemporary world where one must choose one's happiness every day: choose where one lives, choose one's wife, choose whether the children go to state school or private; a world where no social scaffolding can disguise the fact that one's destiny is simply this chameleon stranger, oneself: 'Mimétique malgré lui,' Beckett's Molloy describes himself. Could it be Frank will some day envy Babbo and Mamma? In the kitchen one of two goldfish floats slowly to the surface.

Conformity

'The price to you,' an advert on my local Veronese TV station says, and it uses the singular form – '*il prezzo a te*' – is eighty thousand lire. For a car radio. The price 'to me' I say to myself, and I think: granted the world's an ass, granted one must expect nothing but inanity when one turns on the TV, but why this inanity: the price *to me*? Having said that, I do need a car radio. For our trip to England.

Individuality is at a premium, everything one has is 'personalized', yet in order for us to have everything it must be affordable and so mass-produced. Old yearnings ever at loggerheads. No surprise there. The surprise is rather in the pretending. Why claim that a price is directed at me personally through a medium that notoriously goes out to all and sundry? Like saying 'I love you' to the blind eye of the camera. Why not admit the truth? Standardization.

'You don't have the standard socket,' the shop technician tells me from under the dashboard of my ageing car. The price quoted referred to those who already had the standard socket. Those who were up to date. To *me* it turns out to be considerably higher. But if I'm going to drive a thousand miles and more, I want something to listen to. '95.3 FM,' a pleasant voice tells me as I drive away, 'the station that looks after you.' And again they use the singular form: '*che si cura di te'*. Where did all this begin, I wonder?

We are leaving the day after school closes. I have to pick up my son's report and see his teachers. Michele has good results but – the teachers look very solemn – he has been hitting the other boys. For heaven's sake! 'Can't you discipline him?' But they can't. They are not supposed even to shout at a child, never mind hit him or send him out in the corridor. Discipline is the problem, they say. 'Dead right!' I insist. But one of the women says softly: 'No, you don't understand. Discipline is a problem in the sense that he hits some of the other boys because we can't discipline *them*. Because they make a lot of noise and he says he can't follow the lesson.'

Driving home, I reflect that authority is in retreat all over the Western world: why did I expect my son's elementary school to be any different? If I were invited, I reflect, sitting in my ageing car, to name an expression that is rapidly becoming anachronistic, then the words 'figure of authority' would be among the first to spring to mind. I turn on my new radio, designed especially for me, or rather for my standard socket. Then, in one of those curious ploys of the mind by which one can turn, at least temporarily, the perplexing and potentially alarming – my son is some kind of control freak, or what? – into a pleasure, I decide that I will spend the tedious hours of tomorrow's long drive trying to establish some kind of connection between the fake intimacy of the radio's incessantly repeated 'you', and the erosion of authority in the Cesare Bettelone Elementary School, Montorio, Verona. Only when you have a proper

141

overview, I tell myself, will you be able to confront your son in the appropriate manner. That evening we pack the car in great excitement, and for the moment Michele gets off scot free.

'Without God anything is possible.' The first step is to bring together a quotation or two, marshal one's reading. At 5 a.m., I pick up my ticket for the *autostrada* and hit the accelerator pedal. Certainly my son doesn't believe in God. Understandably. He knows my position and has never been forced to take religious instruction or go to church. Thus he feels safe from divine retribution in a way that I did not at his age. Unlike my younger self, he does not live in terror of eternal hellfire. Hence when thwarted in his creditable desire to follow the lesson, the boy intuitively appreciates Dostoevsky's maxim, takes the law into his own hands and swipes the chatterbox beside him. Why not? Why do I object to this line of action? Because violence is inherently wrong? Or because I feel that it will only bring grief on the boy in the end, knowing as I do that he is not strong enough to impose his will on the class? Is it, then, merely a question of recognizing the limits of one's own power? With the three children dozing in the back, the sky palely bright as the Valpolicella narrows into the Alps, and 95.3 FM doing its best to look after me in thickening traffic, I finally tell my wife what the teachers told me yesterday. 'Michele keeps beating on the kid who sits beside him. A little fellow. Troublemaker, apparently.' She is appalled.

No God, no divine right of kings. No divine right, no legitimate authority. Only power. There is a quote to be had here from a history of the French revolution I was looking at recently: how Napoleon, desperate to establish legitimacy, having no hereditary claim, insisted on his court's being more *moral* than the Bourbons'. Ministers must be accompanied by their legal wives when attending the famous salons, Napoleon insisted. Not their mistresses. The death of conversation, Talleyrand said. I try to think of this while pushing the old car up to 160 k.p.h. in the wild chase of the Italian *autostrada*: a divinely underwritten legitimacy, reaching back to time immemorial, is replaced by a display of propriety. Power based on nothing more now than the mouths of smoking cannons commends itself by cynical adherence to popular notions of piety. With no right, the government must be upright.

But does this connect at all? Am I getting anywhere? And why is legitimacy such a problem? Presumably because without it there can be no recognized authority. No discipline at the Cesare Bettelone school. Upon whose mandate can they spank? Without the divine right of one in particular, every individual has equal rights. Which, once admitted, gives democracy. Everybody decides. But wasn't this supposed to be a good thing?

I get stuck here for a while, caught behind an overtaking truck. I hate the way trucks doing a bare mile an hour more than the trucks in front of them will get in everybody else's way for upwards of ten minutes while they inch past in the fast lane. Until, just beyond Trento, I remember Max Stirner. Of what advantage is it to me to live in a democracy, Stirner asked, or words to that effect, if I disagree with the majority decision? In what way is this different from living under the dictate of a tyrant? Or, to keep our minds on the case in hand: of what use is it to Michele to know he lives in a system which respects individual rights to the point of eliminating punishment, if, as a consequence, he can't follow the lesson? Not all rights can be respected at the same time. 'The truth is,' I tell my wife, rather pleased with this line of thought: 'that one is frequently choosing to "behave" as it were, while deep down holding the conviction that there is no moral reason for doing so. It's just one's lack of clout.' A person's rights are equivalent to his power: thus Spinoza.

Like a merely local divinity, no longer able to take care of me, 95.3 FM fades away to be replaced by accordion-accompanied yodelling. In German. Everything is running smoothly at the Austrian border. Nobody so much as looks into the car to see if we are hiding drugs, or a dangerous subversive. Michele yawns and wakes up. Beyond the barriers there is a patch of tarmac, a small island of right angles attaching ribbons of asphalt that reach out across the wild landscape. A few yards to either side, I tell him, and you would be lost in the icy wilderness where not so long ago they discovered the mummified corpse of Similaun Man: overcome by the cold far from home five thousand years ago. It is dangerous to abandon the group. Stretching our legs in thin cloud at two thousand metres, the children demand I buy them chocolate from the small café. Not yet. Three against two, they insist, casting a proxy vote for baby Lucia who still hasn't woken up. But the family is not a democracy, fatherhood still confers a limited authority. Though it seems I won't be permitted to spank the dear things for much longer. After two thousand years the Pope recently announced that neither the Madonna nor Joseph ever smacked Baby Jesus.

Could it be then, I think, once back on the road, that this brutal truth, my inability to get the quite reasonable things I want, is what prompts society to engage in a constant policy of blandishment? Every public medium seeks to caress my 'individuality', in order to compensate for my all too real submission to the general will. WILLKOMMEN IN ÖSTERREICH, announces a sign, after pistol-toting guards have waved me by.

The road dives deeply into *Sound of Music* valleys and, perhaps because these mountains remind me of the time I worked in Switzerland, the name Helvetius springs to mind, though he was French I think. 'The large states we live in,' Helvetius memorably said, 'are not much interested in awakening the spirit, since they are preserved by virtue of the mass.' It's hard to argue with that, but it scarcely seems a promising preamble to explaining to Michele why he should behave at school: because nobody wants him to become a spirited person. Rousseau on the other hand had a more generous interpretation: 'authority,' says Jean Jacques, 'is imperceptibly substituted by the power of habit: custom, tradition, opinion.' So perhaps all I need do is explain to my son that he should refrain from hitting others for the simple reason that this is *not what pupils do in their classes*, even though they may with impunity break other rules, like the

145

ban on chatter. It's a question of custom. Or rather: Michele, it is more important, don't you see, that you don't hit someone than that you get a good education, because while it is an accepted part of contemporary life not to get a good education it is not acceptable to hit people. We don't object when another country is dull – Switzerland; we do when they go to war – Iraq. But the more I elaborate, the less this seems like the opening I'm looking for.

The road unwinds into the great grain basket of southern Germany. Occasionally, through the trees, or on the distant slopes of low hills, we glimpse wooden spires and painted *Weinstuben*, a sort of discreetly withdrawn national character, while what is mainly present to the hurrying traveller on the autobahn is the standard international fare of black tarmac and white lines. People from a scattering of different nations, all headed to their separate destinations, behave in a standard fashion: indicating, moving out to overtake, indicating, moving back in again. Only when there are roadworks do people really act differently. The German cars all slow down to the indicated speed limit. Less literal-minded, those of us with Italian and French plates keep the foot firmly down. We know that there is no need for custom to correspond exactly to law. A pink Porsche overtakes me, then slows drastically to the limit, which is now a rather tedious 100 k.p.h. When I move out to overtake, he moves out to block me, waving his fist. Ah, but now you're in Germany, I tell myself. So do as the Germans. I sit on the tail of the pink Porsche.

No, as far as my son is concerned, I shall have to come at

this from another angle. I'm getting nowhere. I start again for the twentieth time. God and the divine right meant belief in hereditary authority, went together with ancestor worship, for power was conferred by the Almighty at some point in the past, some point when men and deities communed. Thus, pots in tombs and sacred texts, the individual less important than the continuum to which he belonged. Stasis. In contrast: no God and no divine right means no hereditary authority, no ancestor worship. Rather ashes in the suburban breeze and flavour of the day. Little respect for, or even memory of the past. Provincialism of the contemporary. New bestseller. New video clip. New Labour. Above all, movement. So, the liturgical chant recalling – no, rehearsing – the origins is replaced by the political slogan offering a better future.

A better future. Could this be the key? Approaching Mainz, I feel I might be getting somewhere. The pink Porsche has turned off, we're back at 160 k.p.h. and Rita is playing I-Spy with the children. 'I spy with my little eye something beginning with M.' So: people are persuaded to give their allegiance not by telling them things must be as they are because divinely appointed, but by encouraging them to believe things need not always be as they are. 'Things are not right, far from it; indeed we know that you, as an individual, are unhappy, and above all unable to realize your potential, but those things can be made better. Better for you personally. Submit a bit longer and all will be well.' Ah! 'Is it in the car?' Stefi asks. 'It is,' Rita says. Allegiance, then, not to a present power, but to a process pointing towards the future. Paradise neither past nor lost, but just around the corner. 'Is it made of plastic?' Michele wants to know. 'It is not,' Rita tells him. That is, to spell it out once and for all: I accept this authority not because it is perfect, or even particularly legitimate, but because it recognizes and institutionalizes my unhappiness with the present state of affairs. 'Is it made of metal?' 'It is not.' So Hegel was the guy I should have been thinking of: his history horse galloping across the landscape towards future freedoms, future resolutions of the group–individual conflict. 'We give up,' says Michele. My wife laughs. And I say: Mirror.

Permanent revolution. Life in the near future. Instead of fear of change, society clutches at the principle of change as the only sure, the only legitimate thing it has. Everybody looks together at the rearview mirror in the speeding car where, for one long moment, I meet Michele's eyes and announce:

'By the way, Mick, I heard some pretty bad stuff from your teacher yesterday.'

There is a sudden silence. I turn off the radio.

'You've been hitting this kid who sits next to you. You mustn't do that.'

'But he keeps talking, Dad. During the lesson. He . . .'

'Michele . . .'

'Dad, if I kept on and on talking when you had a guest, you'd smack me, wouldn't you?'

'Damn right I would, but I'm your father, I have power

over you. You don't have power over, what's his name? Rizzitelli.'

'But I want to follow the lesson.'

Suddenly it occurs to me that the whole crisis in contemporary child-rearing has to do with our insistence on articulating explanations. Consider: to bridge the gap between lip-service to individual spirit and *de facto* submission to a mediocre majority I have had to conjure up the dubious vision of a dynamic of improvement mediating between personal discomfiture and group authority. Am I really going to explain Hegelian dialectic to an eleven-year-old?

'When I smack you, Mick, I get what I want, I mean your obedience, because you know you can't avoid my control. But your hitting this Rizzitelli won't get you what you want, because he knows you are not supposed to be in charge of him. On the contrary, since he knows it bothers you, he will chatter all the more and the teachers will give even less importance to his talking, since they find your violence the more disturbing of the two problems. So, even if you're right about wanting to follow the lesson, trying to get that by hitting him will only make matters worse. You have to think about the future, how to really improve things.'

My wife latches on to this and says yes.

'So first, stop hitting people. Ask to talk to the teacher in private. Ask her to bring up the question at the parents' meeting. That way you make it harder for her not to find some way of dealing with Rizzitelli.'

Amazingly, Michele seems submissive and attentive.

'Get other people on your side and the situation can generally be improved,' I insist. 'Especially if you show your willingness to toe the line.'

'That's right,' my wife says.

'Yes, Dad, I'm sorry, Dad.' Michele is shamefaced.

And, incredibly, it seems I've done it. I've done it! Advised my child, secured my wife's approval. Deliriously pleased with this affirmation of modern fatherhood, I then spend the whole trip up the Rhine revelling in the following train of thought:

that the notion of social progress is not unlike the sort of imaginative accounting that allows a parlous situation to acquire just enough credit to keep it lurching from one upset to the next;

that the anguish of the idiot in the pink Porsche arose from his reflection that, if I was speeding, the control he was exercising on his expensively motorized libido was not strictly necessary: he would only behave if everybody else did;

that the vociferous declaration of dissatisfaction together with the tacit acceptance of authority is the conjuring trick of contemporary conformity; this explains how people can crowd into a cinema to see an anti-establishment movie (but every movie is anti-establishment) and *all* agree with it;

that it was a stroke of genius on the part of the moderns to conceal custom in fashion, conformity in nonconformity, in short to institutionalize innovation;

that the fake and creepy intimacy of all public discourse is a direct descendant of the fake and creepy piety Napoleon introduced when he appreciated that an illegitimate government must be a moral one, or be seen to be so; that society doesn't need you, it needs you to behave; that if the mind is, as the Vedic texts imagined, liquid, so that everything flows together in it, still each individual mind is profoundly separate from every other; hence, if the word is the chief mediator between mind and world, mind and mind, conformity must begin with the word: first the liturgical chant, then the political slogan, and now – what progress! – the oft repeated inanity, 'the price to you'.

Late that night, about to emerge from the Channel Tunnel, I discover that the recorded voice wishing me a pleasant onward journey is not only outside my car, on the train's PA, but has locked into my radio as well. There's no escaping. The proof of a theory, I think proudly, is how easily it reproduces itself in everything around us. And, although exhausted by the drive, I am feeling moderately pleased with myself and all in all rather intelligent, when a great wail from the back of the car – Michele has thumped Stefi, because she has pinched Lucy – finally prompts the illumination that makes a mockery of all my reflection: my son hits the boy next to him, I suddenly realize, *because he likes hitting people*. Because he is violent! The business, I realize, about wanting to follow the lesson was doubtless true, but actually only offered an *opportunity* for the conflict he was anyway seeking. People are irrepressibly violent, I tell

151

myself, nerves seriously on edge at the end of this very long trip. I myself would have pushed that stupid prick in the Porsche off the road given half a chance. So my elaborate suggestion of non-violent ways to solve Michele's classroom problem can only lead him to seek other targets for these negative impulses. His sister, for example. She's clutching her elbow now and kicking and screaming. There's a moment of family frenzy. I'm furious, ready to wade in and give the lot of them a bloody good hiding. 'Calm down!' my wife shouts, far from calm herself. Taking a deep breath, I suddenly appreciate that repression is our only hope. The only thing we have got. Constant vigilant repression. Stefi is still whimpering. Hegel is left far behind on the European mainland. I start the car in a well-ordered line of others and, to the friendly adieus of Channel Tunnel Radio, accelerate into the sodium-lit drizzle of the United Kingdom, where they pretend to be different by driving on the left.

Rancour

What the gods most required of man was recognition. But it wasn't enough to extort this with divine manifestations. Already the first to assume human forms, the Olympians complicated matters by appearing as beggars, or strangers: Zeus at the court of Lycaon, Dionysus at the house of Icarius. Certainly it's a tough proposition to treat every panhandler as if he might be God. Clearly one was only a step away from the wearisome modern demand that one recognize the divinity in all men. In this respect it has to be granted that writers are more accommodating. Or you could say rather that they take fewer risks: they rarely turn up without a visiting card. So it was that the day I met V.S. Naipaul his books were everywhere in evidence.

Unrecognized, the gods wreaked the most appalling revenge. But Naipaul had long gone beyond that. He had been awarded the Commonwealth Prize for Literature, hence was firmly placed in the Pantheon. At the conference, where he talked about his work, and then the celebratory lunch where we sat opposite each other, he expressed eloquent opinions on racism and evil authority, earnest comments on his native Trinidad. But what was most evident was how much he was revelling in the buzz of recognition, a god listening to the chatter of human

153

worship. I found him entirely charming. And at the same time couldn't help remarking that in all the writers I have met there is this extraordinary gap between what their work appears to be about – impeccably commendable – and the driving impulse behind it, an unslakable thirst for recognition.

Why did *I* start writing, then? Or, to put it in a slightly more complicated way: how is it that one knew one wanted to be a writer without knowing what writing meant, without appreciating what kind of recognition it was one yearned for? Was there, in the beginning, a clear vision of self as writer: a grown-up, glamorous, guru figure in some foreign villa somewhere? Or simply an impulse: write. How difficult it is to establish this point! All I really know is that, both spiritually and technically, it began with copying. And, notoriously, with copying authors I didn't understand: Samuel Beckett and Henry Green. One could have copied writers one understood better: Graham Greene, Anthony Powell, people whose themes and moral engagement were clear enough. But perhaps it was exactly the combination of being immensely excited by something without in the least understanding it that drew me to Beckett and Green. They were divinities for me. I was in their thrall. How many years would it be before I realized that this is the only relationship a writer really wants with his readers?

At the university we were allowed to submit a piece of 'creative writing' for possible bonus points in our final exams. I wrote a few pages entitled 'The Three of Us'. My first production. It was dismissed with a D. Curiously, I cannot recall being greatly upset by this. I simply thought: *One day I shall bury you all.* Was this the first time I framed those words for myself, words since repeated, though rarely shared, a thousand times? I cannot recall. But no doubt it was the same sense of self against the world that, again without for a moment understanding why, responded so warmly to the unexpected and unchristian outbreaks of Beckett's narrators. I remember in particular a few lines in *From an Abandoned Work*: 'Whereas a bird now, or a butterfly, fluttering about and getting in my way, all moving things, getting in my path, a slug now, getting under my feet, no, no mercy.' And he hits out with his stick. Or there is the brutal clarification that closes the first paragraph of *Malone Dies*: 'Let me say before I go any further, that I forgive nobody.'

That writing is a phenomenon often galvanized by anger is evident enough. How rancorous Shakespeare's plays are! How Hamlet raves and Lear rages! And Swift and Pope and Byron, and Dickens too in his way. Only those who do not understand what a central part such emotions play in life, could consider Eliot's description of *The Waste Land* as 'one long rhythmical grumble' reductive. What is not so clear is the nature of the writer's rancour, where it came from, what it is about. Could it be this matter is taboo?

The Cambridge Board of Examiners failed to discourage me. After a few postgrad months at Harvard I tired of studying other people's writing and embarked myself on a novel. It went through a very distinct Beckettian phase, followed by a very distinct Greenian phase. Perhaps not

155

insignificantly it was called 'The Bypass'. I gave it to a lady
tutor who found a very kind way of telling me she thought
it awful. I remember her asking me why I so obsessively
used demonstratives and disorientating word orders. The
answer, of course, which I didn't give, was that Green used
them. But at the time I had no idea why. The divinities I
was copying were a foreign land to me. I was like someone
repeating words in a language that, not only does he not
know, but is not even learning. *I shall bury you all*, I
thought, leaving this nice lady tutor's house. I must have
been past thirty before it occurred to me that precisely this
angry impulse was the foreign country I had been setting
out to discover. And it wasn't foreign at all. Just dark.
'Luke,' says Darth Vader, 'you do not know the power of
the dark side.' And how right he is.

Over lunch that day, Naipaul claimed that he knew he
was going to be a writer from the beginning. He would
never have done anything else. Not even temporarily. Not
even part time. He was a writer and that was that. I
remarked that if they hadn't published him, he would have
been obliged to do something else. Wouldn't he? An
animated discussion then developed as to whether it was
possible for a writer of talent not to be recognized. And if I
insisted, enlisting Thomas Gray, that it was indeed possible,
then this no doubt was out of the same immodesty that
inspired Naipaul to insist that it was not. He genuinely
could not imagine a world where his genius would not be
recognized. In this he showed himself more confident than
the Olympians. But I was thinking of the years between

1979 and 1985. A bedsit in Acton. Two rooms rented from a retired Pole in Kensal Rise. A novel called 'Promising', never published; a novel called 'Leo's Fire', never published; a novel called 'Quicksand'. Never published. A novel called 'Failing'. Never published. Enough rejection slips to paper Buckingham Palace. 'It is a gesture of religious faith, religious faith,' I insisted – growing extremely heated and perhaps rather shrill – 'to assume that we live in a world where everything receives its just desserts.' Naipaul smiled and, very charmingly, changed the subject. Clearly he did have a religious faith. In himself. For which I envy him.

Those who are most easily and swiftly successful – and so ultimately have less opportunity to develop – are those whose innate anger is skilfully and unimpeachably directed at what is widely perceived to be a proper object of anger. Aside from all the politically engaged fiction the English have produced this century and last, one recalls with some amusement the year three of the six shortlisted novels for the Booker Prize found cause to feature the Holocaust. Sadly, this honourable directing of negative energy has never worked for me. I did once translate a book by a survivor of Birkenau. But though I sometimes wept as I transcribed what I had to, I could never feel as much anger towards the Nazis as one feels, on occasion, for the obtuseness of a colleague, or wife, or child, or editor. Or indeed for Naipaul's complacency over that lunch. One's condemnation, no, one's horror of torturers, murderers, exploiters of every kind is so automatic and complete that it hardly seems worth dramatizing. What would that bring us

157

aside from the reassuring reflection that we still feel 'the right way' about things? 'I have written a very angry novel,' a contemporary tells me in the Café Rouge on the Old Brompton Road. And he begins to give me the details of the Nestlé scandal. As if the point of *Hamlet* were that 'there is something rotten in the state of Denmark'. The newspapers would have told us that.

It was not so much that I was undiscouraged in those early years, as undeterred. Humiliation seems to spur me on. The more birds and butterflies and ducks ('ducks are the worst,' says Beckett) get in my path, the more wildly I flail about with my stick. Even though, if I look back, it is with some amazement that I see myself embarking on – what? – the sixth novel, the seventh, with each collecting twenty, perhaps thirty letters of rejection. Perhaps my wife's faith was important. So much so that one wonders now if one will ever be able to forgive her the generous and self-effacing part she played in what was about to become a career. For finally, perhaps convinced that I was never to be published, I turned my attention to my family, some events in my childhood. And at last the breakthrough came, and came where, in terms of personal relationships, it was most embarrassing. Before its acceptance, however, that novel too went through the familiar round of rejection letters; to kill the meantime I concocted a crime thriller which hinged on the irony that while the hero, desperate for some kind of recognition, condemns the world for its obtuseness, he himself becomes involved in theft, kidnap and murder. Clearly the fellow is loathsome, as the Olympians likewise were hardly fair in obliterating people who could not see that a beggar was a god. Yet character and circumstance were so manipulated in this dark comedy that it was hard not to feel that the protagonist was right about those around him, and that in a way a world so stubbornly complacent could expect little better than to find itself castigated by such an anti-hero. I finished this exercise in displaced rancour at about the time the novel based on my family came out. The latter was generally applauded for its exposure of a gauche and potentially harmful kind of evangelism. Apparently its heart was in an acceptable place. Only a decade later, when it was published in Italy, did I have the shock of coming across a reviewer who put a shrewder finger on the matter: 'This novel', he wrote, 'has the assurance of someone with a smile of revenge on his lips. He who observes and proves able to tell his story is always the winner over those unable to tell.'

How eager the world is to set up writers and artists on their pedestals! The Pulitzer. The Booker. The Prix Goncourt. To see them as a force for good. The Commonwealth Prize. The Nobel Prize! Inherently liberal, liberating! The courageous writers of Eastern Europe under Communism! What a gift the Rushdie affair has been for the person who endorses this kind of vision! The writer as a champion of human freedom! When the irony is that, beside the criminal, the artist is the first to take liberties, often at the expense of others, as Rushdie took (and I have taken, indeed even now am taking) a lot of liberties with what others hold sacred. The artist is the first to appropriate

159

the world for his own purposes. Implicitly, often unconsciously, he claims direct contact with some absolute that lies beyond the public good. However much lip-service may be paid at celebratory lunches.

Michelangelo, as we know, was convinced that the figures he sculpted were already present in the rock. He merely used his chisel to expose them. Wasn't this, like Naipaul's, a religious faith? In himself. The world was *as he saw it*. If matter wasn't simply submitting to his genius, then in some way it was co-penetrative with it. Self annexes other and annuls it. How absurd! Yet if you'd been there at the first unveiling of his David, stood stunned in the piazza before a muscular beauty that had all the elegance and clarity of classical proportion, but throbbing too with a wholly new and vibrant sense of life, you wouldn't have argued with the artist. You wouldn't have wanted to sift through the lumps and shards on his studio floor to see whether there mightn't have been some different, perhaps even better sculpture to be made from that same piece of rock. For you are convinced, seduced, dazzled. Michelangelo is right, you say, this is how life is, the figure was in the rock.

Art is coercive. It rearranges our mental space, imposes a vision. Rational argument is bypassed, forgotten. So that with the best art one suffers a sense of inevitability – which is exactly the experience of the seduced at the moment they succumb. How can one open a novel of Thomas Bernhard and not be immediately and completely compelled by what suddenly seems the *only* possible response to a world wallowing in hypocrisy? How can one read the 'Ode to a

160

Grecian Urn' without feeling, while the enchantment lasts, that this is the perfect, ultimate and *only* important statement on the relationship between mortal man and immortal artefact?

Art is 'liberating' in the sense that it frees you from the grip of whatever other vision you were previously in thrall to. Subjecting you to another. In a process not unlike the now popular serial monogamy. Thus Beckett seduced me, Green seduced me. No one made English prosody more triumphantly his own than Henry Green, with his strange deployment of articles and demonstratives, the bizarre but entirely convincing way he could make life regenerate itself around his wayward syntax. What I had sought to copy, then, in those early days, without being at all aware of it, was a powerful act of seduction. One man's making the world in his own image, declaring it thus. As a greenhorn might copy a Casanova. Or Zeus a Titan. This to compel the recognition that I had been compelled to give to others. One might, looking back now, have sought to gain it merely by offering people what one thought they wanted. Pleasing the crowd. And perhaps I have tried this from time to time. But the truth is that at the very best such a policy can only bring praise. Not recognition. For real recognition involves the reader's wholehearted endorsement of my, truly *my* vision. Not his consumption of something he already knew he wanted. What god would ever pander to the way man saw things? What mortal, in the long run, would feel happy with so accommodating a divinity? Thus the only important reading experiences are those where one

161

set out with scepticism, only to find ourselves enchanted, overwhelmed by a vision that demands our acquiescence. And one's problem, perhaps, when first one sets out to write, is that one doesn't really have anything so grand as a vision. Few ever do. So one copies, learning hopefully from the tension between oneself and one's model. Later it will be a question of learning not to copy yourself.

But we have still to place that rancour. For it is only rudely disguised in righteous anger, only crudely parodied in reductive comedies about criminal fellows who cannot bear the world's not being as they would wish it, that long list of literary villains, so close, one always feels, to their creators. At that celebratory lunch, Naipaul politely enquired about my own writing and I made the mistake of concluding my brief reply with the self-regarding remark that: 'The reviewers are generally kind.' He was on to this weakness in a flash. 'You read reviews, then?' he asked. 'I never do. After all,' he smiled, 'one knows the quality of one's work without them.' And what has occurred to me, mulling over this conversation through the years, is that one of the problems every divinity must face is this: why do I *care* to be recognized by these people who are inherently incapable of appreciating my true worth? Why bother with their reviews? And all that anger the gods displayed when recognition wasn't forthcoming, mightn't it perhaps have been at least partly directed against themselves for having wanted such a ludicrous thing in the first place? Could it be that Naipaul was unhappy with how happy he was to be lionized at conference lunches? A situation he would doubtless have satirized were he writing about it. Was he furious, perhaps, to find himself *human*? Is this the artist's true pathos? One creates a world and *still* one is human. Is this the source of all his rancour? Or might we alternatively suggest that Naipaul's withdrawal, his not reading reviews, was made possible precisely by the fact that the world was seeking him out. He was already recognized. In this sense perhaps we guarantee a god's absence when we praise him with regularity. For few divinities will bother to go on manifesting themselves once their supremacy is established. Most notoriously Jehovah. What we will never know is whether this recognition has reconciled them to their existence.

It is in his dealings with the public that the ambiguity and essential fragility of the writer's position is revealed. When Rousseau's Thérèse bore him children, he immediately had them removed and deposited at the local foundling hospital, nor does this appear to have caused him any great suffering. But when a musical score he had written was rejected, he recalls: 'Deeply distressed at receiving this verdict in place of the praises I had expected, and which were certainly due to me, I returned home sick at heart. Tired out and consumed by grief, I fell ill and for six weeks was not fit to leave my room.' But one needn't look so far to see that behind, or perhaps I mean alongside, all that is beautiful and moving in art, all that is genuinely worthy, all that truly opens the heart and lifts the spirit, lies a suffocated scream for recognition. A London paper's diary tells me how, on receiving a miserable review, Jeanette Winterson went along to the reviewer's house and shouted abuse at her on her doorstep. A contemporary describes a party where he was harangued by Malcolm Bradbury for a bad review he had written two years before. An editor tells me how the great Thomas Bernhard wrote to his paper demanding to be reviewed because he was, in his own words, 'the best novelist since the war'. And even the marvellous Calasso once asked me to translate a letter for him in which he complained about a virulent and obtuse review he had received. Though of course he never sent it. For the truth is that a divinity does not and must not stoop to such things. If one has (alas!) no thunderbolt at one's disposal, a lofty silence is the only resource. Though offhand I can think of two writers who have killed themselves for lack of recognition: Richard Burns in England, Guido Morselli in Italy. If you have the stomach for it, a gesture of that kind will certainly compel some to take you seriously.

Gloucester to Prospero. Gabriel to Anna Livia. Belacqua to the Unnameable. That there is a natural trajectory in a writer's production seems obvious enough. One begins in a whirlwind of describing telling evoking. The world is so fresh, so interesting, so urgently in need of our engagement. But once the most obvious material is exhausted, what then? My first unpublished attempt, 'The Bypass' was all spoken in the northern intonations of my infancy. I was then weary of that. My first published novel spoke of the Christian charismatic movement in the sixties. I could hardly tackle that again. The second featured an office in Acton where I had worked, a secret love affair. Acton is not a place to revisit and one secret love affair is surely enough. So on and on. Marriage will offer much material. Children. In my case people write to me regularly asking for a third book on Italy. But I feel Italy has had more than its fair share of my attention. One can of course go out and seek material. A novel about Christ's disciples? A novel about the moon landings? But after this has been done once or twice? There comes a point where the mind grows more interested in the way it deals with materials than in the materials themselves. For there have been so many. Or rather, the mind begins to appreciate that the materials cannot be understood separately from its own operations upon them. It starts to claim hegemony, demand the upper hand. There is an entirely natural inward-turning in a writer's later development. Not a withdrawal from action, but a penetration of what lies behind all action: the seductive, luminous, coercive, shadowy, genial, and rancorous mind.

Henry Green stopped writing in his fifties. A heavy drinker, he seems to have spent most of his time running the family company or chasing women. His favourite activity he described as 'romancing over a bottle'. Joyce turned away from evocation of the world to evocation of the processes by which a world is evoked. Beckett steadily peeled voice from voice, posture from posture, heading for silence at the same speed as the frog who always jumps half the distance that remains between himself and his goal. No one better than he dramatizes the irony that while the sort of consciousness writing encourages is one that counsels suspicion of self and of words, still one wishes to be

165

recognized for having articulated that fact. 'No future here,' comments the narrator of *Worstward Ho.* And goes on: 'Alas yes.' But for recognition of the artist's essential rancour and its intimate relation to his genius for coercion, the greatest example remains *The Tempest,* a title that speaks worlds. People like to forget what an angry, punitive, even cynical fellow Prospero is. How quickly he dismisses his daughter's brave new world! 'One more word shall make me chide thee, if not hate thee,' he tells Miranda when she appeals for Ferdinand's life. His magician's spells, however beautiful, are designed to bind not please. And if, unlike Malone, Prospero does at the end forgive, how grudgingly it is done. And that only when every enemy is dead or in his power, only when the gesture of relinquishing power provides the final claim to superiority, the ultimate demand for recognition.

'Style' – thus Proust, in *Contre Sainte-Beuve* – 'is the transformation thought imposes on reality.' I'm at my desk. About to start again. To attempt that transformation again. What shall I write about? Two or three reviews of my last novel concurred in describing the main character as 'unappealing'. Dear, dear. As Richard III, as Prospero, as Raskolnikov, as Mr Rock, as Molloy, Moran, Malone. People like to forget. But appealingly aware of being unappealing, I had thought. And aware again of how little awareness helps. I stare at the screen. Shall we proceed with this tail-chasing? Aware of wishing to claim recognition for being aware that an appealing awareness of being unappealing does not help? A deep breath. Writing, I tell myself, staring at the screen, involves a complex movement of the spirit in which one is simultaneously aware of the most sublime and the most base. Another deep breath. The impulse to comfort and the impulse to truth were ever at loggerheads, I reflect, still wincing from those reviews. Another breath. 'Impose' surely, I remind myself, is the key word in Proust's formulation – the transformation thought *imposes* on reality. Again a breath. Until all at once, birds in my path! Ducks! A great flapping and squawking. For I'm reminded of how at the end of that famous lunch with Naipaul I heard the author lean over and say softly to his official hostess that his expenses claim would be arriving shortly. All moving things in my path! Although it seemed he'd arrived chauffeur-driven in a car they'd sent some considerable distance for him. What other expenses could he possibly have? And gossiping over this matter with others at the conference, as (however unappealingly) one will, I discovered that the great man was a stickler for expenses. A terrible stickler. Down to the very last penny, I was told. And had been paid for his performance too! Whereas my little talk merely allowed me to waive some paltry fees. Oh, but how well sour grapes can be relied upon to stir the soul! Have at you, quackers! A great flourish of the stick. Or wand. I shall bury you all, I decide. Let's write about love!

Analogies

On a Sunday afternoon in October 1996, Verona lost their first home fixture of the season, two-nil to Bologna, and this was also the day that Giorgio told me his marriage was on the rocks. We were in the Curva-Sud, the end where the hardcore fans hang out, and there was a great deal of excitement before the game, for it was the first of our return from the provincial gloom of Serie B to the city swank of Serie A. There were banners and fireworks, high hopes, stirring chants: followed by great disappointment. Usually a game of football, like a marriage, can be seen in at least two ways. But not this one. Verona were unfit and uninspired. I can't remember a single shot on goal. Bologna were kind to score only two. Shuffling out afterwards, Giorgio told me in confidence that he was renting a separate apartment. He had never loved his wife, he said. My son, a stalwart twelve-year-old, wept and kicked the steps. Giorgio's slightly older daughter was stoical with a smile. For the next eight months the four of us were bound together by our season tickets.

Notoriously fickle, memory seems to have two modes: the overall impression, which is an unverifiable sediment, and the episode: visual or audio replay. It's remarkable how little interplay there is between these two. Thus the following game against Cagliari was overwhelmingly dull,

168

but the episodes I recall are very positive: our laughably lucky first equalizer, deflected off a defender, the brilliant second, low drive first time after high cross. Marriage counsellors say that one negative experience wipes out at least four positive, leaving no favourable sediment. Certainly Giorgio at this point could remember absolutely nothing happy about his fifteen-year marriage. But I hoped that one point snatched from Cagliari – the first after three successive defeats, one home, two away – might turn the tide. My son, Michele, thought we deserved more. Maria Giulia proclaimed it a fair result. And her father dropped her off at home. She had been told that work obliged him to live a while in Florence.

I want to establish a difference between fidelity and faith, in football and in love. I came to the city of Verona by purest chance. An Italian girl who found me at a party in Boston had a brother who studied medicine here and so was able to offer us his apartment for a week when we were married. Thus the Yellow-blues became my team. And though one might sometimes have wished to support Milan, Juventus, Inter, the kind of team who could give you a championship or trounce Bayern Munich, still one is never unfaithful. It's not another team you want, but for your own to be successful. '*In Italia Hellas*' we sing – for officially the club's called Hellas Verona – '*in Europa Hellas*'. And the chant ends '*e ovunque Hellas è sempre gialloblù*'. What fidelity! Everywhere Hellas! Always Yellow-blue. But without faith, for none of us remotely believes we will get into Europe again, never mind anywhere else.

Giorgio said the point was he hadn't really chosen his wife. It had all been an accident that happened when they were very young. Therefore it was quite reasonable that he should now have another passion: banally, his secretary. But he hadn't got her to move into his apartment. Eighteen years younger than himself, Raffaella lived at home with parents who would be shocked. Also there was a boyfriend still to be discarded. And so he would be, she said, when Giorgio made it quite clear what he wanted. Giorgio spent his evenings walking in the suburban cold and discussing things on his mobile phone with his girlfriend and his wife. 'Don't tell the children anything until I've decided,' he said.

Perversely, one of the pleasures of football is the gap that so often opens up between what one deserves and what one gets. Thus despite some improved play, the draw with Cagliari proved to be a false dawn. We played a very solid game against Inter in mid-November, only to see them go ahead in the last minute and completely against the run of play with a brilliant individual goal by Javier Zanetti. During the second half I had to scold my son for joining in the racist chants against Inter's three black players. Giorgio was disgusted. 'We didn't deserve that,' he said. I didn't tell him that his wife had used almost the same words, indeed the same cadence, to tell me how she felt about his desertion.

Marina had called on a number of occasions and finally came round to visit. Overdressed, she tried to be cynically bright, but was constantly on the point of tears. She wanted to understand, she said. For if Giorgio had another woman he would have told her. He had sworn he didn't have another woman. Embarrassed, I said something about men finding this period of life difficult. Apparently Giorgio would come home for a couple of days, cry, then go away again. And each time he went away it was for longer. She felt she did not deserve this. She was paying a terribly high price for the children she had had, who had made her less attractive. But she had faith, she said. She could not believe he would not come back. He was a good man. She knew he was. I felt that, far from being unattractive, she was a beautiful woman. It seems some nights she left the children on their own and stayed out till two or three.

When one flicks through the TV channels and comes upon a game of football it is very hard not to stop and watch, then harder still not to take sides. Likewise when couples one knows turn their lives into a battle. Watching the TV, rather than rooting *for* one of the two teams, one tends to root *against* the other. And this is the essential difference between our emotional response to football at the stadium and football at home: that since our own team rarely appears on the TV, we are almost always rooting *against* a team, rather than for our own. You want pain for one side, usually the most powerful and famous, rather than pleasure for another. All of a sudden, I found that, although Giorgio was my friend, although I had often nodded in agreement with his complaints about his wife, although, above all, we went to watch Verona together, to suffer together that is, through a miserable season, somehow I was rooting *against* him. Was I jealous? Of his younger woman?

171

Did I want him to get his come-uppance? The way I felt about the neighbouring provincial team Vicenza, who were far higher in the table than they deserved. It was disquieting.

Our first victory came against Roma. After the previous week's away defeat at Reggiana ('lowly Reggiana,' an English sports reporter would say) there had been talk in the papers about certain players not trying hard enough, not honouring their yellow-blue shirts. I felt this was unfair. Why would they not try hard? 'Happy is my lot in life,' says Kierkegaard, 'if my wish coincides with my duty.' And surely this is almost always true for a footballer. For why on earth would he not wish to win? Which is his duty. Marina's wishes also seemed to coincide with her duty: loving her husband and children. 'Most people's task in life,' Kierkegaard notes, 'is to bow to their obligation and by their enthusiasm to transform it into their wish.' In this sense Giorgio's wife, like the indignant Verona players interviewed by the local paper, could claim that, however badly things were going, she was happy with herself.

Not so Giorgio. Before the game he began to weep over the question of his children, though he did it softly so that with the noise of the crowd Maria Giulia would not hear. It was a bracing cold winter day and she was tearing up her programme to make paper planes. At the same time he was in love with Raffaella. Or believed he was. He then spoke earnestly of having a duty to *himself*: to live life to the full. He was in danger of dying without realizing any of his potential to love, without really having lived. But this sounded very much like reason being brought in after the event to drag duty kicking and screaming in a direction where it was not inclined to go. Or as dictators pay apologists to legitimize their *coups d'état*. Otherwise, where was the conflict? Michele said if we lost this one as well he would tear up his season ticket and chuck it on to the pitch.

Amazingly Verona scored first. With the help of a very dubious piece of refereeing Rome got an equalizer. But football, like the mind, is ever fluid. Like wayward thoughts, players head off in the most unexpected directions, there are sudden fizzes of conflict, then the patterned felicity of things coming together there where it seemed – and this is endemic with Verona – there was only confusion. Two passes, three, four, and suddenly two perfect triangles lay end to end. Verona had scored again. Ragged and incredulous, the boys soaked up the pressure and hung on, not without some heroic goalkeeping. For the first time the crowd stood for a roaring ovation. Mixed with chants of '*Roma, Roma, vaffanculo!*' which corresponds, I suppose, to 'Fuck off Rome.' Ageing idol and goal scorer, Toto De Vitis came to salute the crowd. How we shrieked and worshipped him. How we love our players when they win! When they allow us to shout triumphant insults at opposing crowds. The terraces were a sea of flags. I love that. Giorgio, who had bellowed throughout, had a beatific smile. 'Maybe I won't leave home after all,' he laughed. Such is the uplifting effect of a good win on the emotions. But the following week Verona lost two-nil away to lowly, very lowly Piaccaza.

There are those who will eagerly tell you of the intelligence of their soccer idols. I remember hearing this of Cantona, and likewise Platini and Lineker. Whereas the truth is that we adore these men for what they can do for our team and not for an off-field intelligence probably inferior to that of almost everybody we despise: politicians, I mean, and coaches too sometimes. Ours certainly. Giorgio, however, would not hear of any suggestion that his young Raffaella was not an unusually intelligent woman. She was simply the most perceptive and acute person he had ever spent time with. 'Intelligently pert breasts?' I enquired. 'Perceptively warm thighs?' As we spoke the P.A. thundered out the tune that accompanies, at least a dozen times before every game, a long commercial for the Cesare Ragazzi Hair Replacement Method. The big screen opposite the Curva-Sud showed a once bald man, apparently Cesare himself, now able to enjoy the pleasures of embracing a naked girl in an underwater scenario which allows us to see just how long and thick transplanted hair can be. The commercialization of mid-life crisis can rarely have been cruder, nor the target audience more appropriate. What do men come to football for if not to revisit their youth? There is an oneiric quality to it all. And it occurred to me, as Michele and Maria Giulia demanded a Coca-Cola, that perhaps young girls do get to seem more cerebral as middle-aged men go soft in the head. Giorgio shook his, poring over the match programme. It lamented that De Vitis was too old to last out the ninety minutes now. And he was eight years younger than either of us. The deserted Marina, I thought, was nothing if not an intelligent woman.

This was the game against Udinese. December the 23rd. After beating Rome we had continued to lose our away games and drawn twice at home, against Vicenza and Sampdoria. Already there was more than a little talk about relegation. Already our coach, Cagni, was striking that attitude of he who has faith despite all evidence to the contrary. Not unlike Marina, still undeceived as to the affair with Raffaella. It was rumoured a sweeper was to be bought from some German team to bolster our miserable defence. Or perhaps it was more a question of keeping up supporters' hopes. Certainly psychology was becoming an important issue, as each week's programme pointed out. Not that anyone was claiming we were one of the more skilled teams in Serie A. But if only the boys could get their heads together, they were not so unskilled as to be lost without a fight. Giorgio told me he was going home for a week for Christmas. One had to be with the children at Christmas, he explained: Maria Giulia and her two younger brothers. Raffaella would be with her boyfriend. Though very much in love with Giorgio, she was finding it difficult to fire her *fidanzato* until invited to share her life with her lover. Perhaps Marina is right to have faith, I thought. Perhaps Cagni is right. There is hope. And in a goal-mouth scramble Udinese scored.

Was this the first game when it occurred to me how problematic the psychology of the season must be for Orlandini, Zanini, Maniero? Still young and at the height of

175

their considerable powers, lent to Verona by big-name teams that had no place for them, these three rising stars must have felt at once frustrated by the mediocrity of their companions and at the same time assured that when the débâcle came they would escape to some other team. The way in a faltering marriage men can feel relieved that at forty-five it will be easier for them to start again than for their wives. Or the way beautiful and intelligent girls know they will come out of a torrid affair better than their ageing lovers. Orlandini and Zanini played well in flashes, as if eager to remind potential buyers of their qualities. But can one commit everything while preparing to bail out? Were the newspapers right to wonder if some were doing less than their level best? Giorgio would be checking out how life felt at home, he said at half-time, but didn't plan to stay when the Christmas holiday was over. The referee was '*venduto*', Michele grumbled, 'paid off'. He hadn't given us an obvious penalty. I felt guilty for having got him into the habit of supporting such a useless team.

Still, it's never over till it's over. There was the second half. Almost at once a brisk break by Orlandini. Perfectly driven cross and Zanini's diving header. Goal! What rapture. Followed not two minutes later by Udinese's second. Really, how could our defence be so bad? There was a definitely unseasonable swelling of frustration and rancour on the terraces now. Hatred of Udinese, whose fans had brought a drum along and banged it loudly, hatred of the team for being so incredibly awful, hatred of ourselves for supporting them, for knowing that we would go on supporting them even after this game. But these too are the emotions you pay for, and which allow you to be more detached and non-combative through the week, even to stave off an argument or two with the wife. With a team like this to hate, I told Giorgio, how can you possibly see your wife in anything but the most positive light? He frowned. Maniero was brought down in the box and we had a penalty. Orlandini. Goal.

Two-all. The winter light had gone. The floodlights came on. Perhaps the approach of Christmas made the crowd suspect a miracle. For Verona – and this is so rare – had begun to attack. There was one of those great rising waves of hope one comes to recognize in crowds and which serve, if nothing else, to remind you that much is still inexplicable. Do players really have more energy because so urgently cheered and encouraged? For no particular reason everyone was shrieking, '*Su! Su!*' 'Up! Up!' Meaning, upfield, but they might have been inciting a corpse to rise from the dead. Appropriately, old Toto was wheeled on, our last-minute substitution. And in the dying seconds of what was now a suspiciously long injury time this declining star, comet I might say, gave us our Christmas present. He had the shrewdness to dummy a low cross on the edge of the six-yard box. The goalkeeper, already diving at him, was completely thrown, and big Maniero was there behind to slide it in. I have never seen my son so ecstatic. Though he claims to hate girls, he was hugging the rather attractive Maria Giulia, lifting her up and plonking her down. He's a big boy. When the floodlights went out, the crowd remained and lit their cigarette lighters as if they were so many candles at a carol service. '*Adesso suona il tamburo!*' they were singing to the tune of 'Guantanamera'. 'Now bang your drum!' The players threw their shirts into the terraces, and one his shorts. And when I got home I felt so happy to see the Christmas tree and my children and my wife, and to think that all was well, I wept.

Counsellors who try to save marriages insist that communication is the first step. Getting each side to tell the other, honestly, how they feel. Without being sure whether this is in fact wise, I've often observed how opposing groups of fans offer a triumphant image of a thoroughly enjoyed non-comprehension. We yell '*Milan, Milan, vaffanculo!*' at the top of our voices. But no sooner have we begun than they are whistling. Drowning us out. Or raising similar chants. So that each fan hears only what he wants to hear. He hates the other team and their fans. Everything around him confirms this hatred. Not unlike those situations where one complains about one's partner to a best friend who eagerly agrees and hopefully follows through with similar grouches of his own. And, at the stadium, so long as both sides remember the theatricality of it all, so long as formal arrangements keep them well apart, this is an enormous, if infantile pleasure, far greater than some intelligent discussion of the game with an opposing fan, perhaps involving the painful admission that his side is in fact infinitely superior to yours. But although it would be reductive to say that football doesn't matter, it's clear that some things matter more. There are areas of life in which the painful admission is appropriate. Thus Marina had used Christmas to tell Giorgio that she appreciated that she shared a great deal of responsibility for what had gone wrong with their marriage and was eager to put that right, eager to love him better, eager to return to what she insisted had been happy years for both of them. Remember this, Giorgio, she said. Remember that. Her generosity took my friend rather by surprise. And frightened him, I think. His response was to stay away from home for almost a month.

What a gloomy month it was! On the high of the Udinese victory we went to our first away game. Atalanta, the Bergamo team. In the coach the fans sang '*Autogrill, Autogrill Autogrill!*' to the tune they usually use to chant a darling player's name. An *autogrill* is a motorway service station. Stopping at one – though the trip from Verona to Bergamo is only an hour and a half – the fans mobbed the café and threw snowballs at accompanying police cars. On the field Verona defended throughout, as if you could ever improve your lot in football without scoring, while a couple of hooligans tried to scale the huge fence they'd put us behind to toss fireworks at the well-to-do Bergamaschi in their better seats. The police didn't miss the chance to use their truncheons. The temperature was below zero. And of course Atalanta bundled in a goal five minutes from time. Everybody was disgusted. 'This is helping you to grow up,' I told my son, casting about for some compensation. 'It's important to get used to losing in life. It's important to learn to stick with things. Through thick and thin.' Giorgio

179

grunted. I could almost hear Kipling. Maria Giulia hadn't wanted to come.

The only reason they hadn't fired our execrable coach Cagni, a well-informed fan told us before the game with Milan, was that they would still have to pay out his contract for the rest of the season. Plus the new arrival's, whoever he was. And Verona didn't have that kind of money. Giorgio too was being forced to count the cost of paying off an old contract. Both he and Marina had been to lawyers. Offer and counter-offer. She wanted three million lira a month. He was going to be relatively poor, he said. Money, we reflected gloomily, was an all-conditioning factor in life. We were watching the list of Milan's players go up on the screen: Maldini, Albertini, Baresi, Boban, Savicevic, Baggio. Even the players they had on the bench were worth more than twice Verona's whole squad put together. And they had changed their coach the minute things started going wrong. The great Sacchi was back. What hope for our Verona?

The ground was packed. But on this occasion the crowd hardly inspired confidence. For one of the galling things about supporting a provincial team in Italy is that the stadium is only truly full when one of the big three comes along: Juventus, Inter, Milan. And it is not that it fills with fans from the big cities themselves, though there are those, nor of locals who are more inclined to pay when there are serious skills to be seen, though there are those too. No, the stadium fills above all with locals who actually *support* one of the big three, born and bred Veronese who wave Juventus flags, sport Inter scarves, wear Milan shirts. These people, happily bereft of any sense of pathos, only support successful teams, mainly on television of course, the way some men only have eyes for the most beautiful and glamorous women. And when the opportunity arises, they have their fling. Though doing so in one's own back yard, so to speak, is hardly in the best of taste. 'We know your names!' the Verona hardcore shrieked. 'We have your addresses.' '*Vergogna*!' Giorgio yelled. 'Shame on you!'

Anyway, it was only a matter of time, I warned Michele. How can a plain and muddling workhorse, like Verona, hold its own against all that glitz? Michele nodded stoically. 'Just enjoy watching the real thing,' I insisted, doubtless more nervous than he was. And Milan did play so beautifully, so sinuously. All those patterned passes. Two, three, four shots on goal. Just a matter of time. Until suddenly, remarkably, our own Orlandini was breaking from a Milan corner. Dribbled Baggio. The whole field before him. Cross to Zanini. Goal. Milan were surprised, but barely worried. The game settled down again into wave after wave of sophisticated attack. Perhaps ten missed opportunities. Until another break. A muddle in the goalmouth. Goal! Two-nil. And just in case we still didn't believe it, they scored again. Orlandini. Our third and last shot of the game. *In Italia Hellas, in Europa Hellas!* What rapture. As the Veronese Milanisti left early in disappointment, the Curva-Sud rose as one man, or rather as one triumphant wife, shaking a fist of good-riddance at defeated whoredom.

'Too bad Maria Giulia wasn't here,' I said afterwards. 'Why's that?' And Giorgio, who hadn't talked about his situation for some time, explained that it was no longer credible to tell the children that he was working in Florence and could only make it home Sundays. So he was now telling them he'd had to go to Rome for a month. Despite the business with the lawyers, it seems the kids still hadn't been informed of the break-up. 'And you haven't asked Raffaella to move in?' 'No.' 'So what are you doing?' Giorgio said he was paralysed until he could come to some decision. 'If you don't make one soon, someone else will make one for you.' How easy it is to give advice! He said he knew that, but it didn't help. Parting, we embraced and I felt mildly ashamed for having rooted against him. The important thing was to sort the situation out, I said. If Verona could beat Milan, there was always hope. 'Perhaps it'll go to penalties,' he said.

The peculiarity of the 'knight of faith', as described by Kierkegaard in *Fear and Trembling*, is that, like 'the knight of infinite resignation' he has made the spiritual gesture of accepting that his wishes cannot be fulfilled, the gesture of renunciation, but unlike him he then goes one step further. Paradoxically, he still believes he will have what he cannot: immortality impossible, yet it will be mine. And it is this paradox, Kierkegaard says, that condemns he who has real faith to the 'martyrdom of unintelligibility'. Certainly Marina was becoming hard to understand when she spoke, quite serenely and practically now, about arrangements for their separation while at the same time explaining that she was convinced Giorgio would come back to her. Certainly Cagni seemed at best incoherent when, in an unforgivably relaxed interview with the local TV station, he claimed that although he was perfectly aware that we were likely to go down, and was resigned to facing that when it came, he nevertheless firmly believed it wouldn't happen. We would win our last games and stay up. It will be noble enough, I thought, if Michele and I become 'knights of infinite resignation'. 'Don't hope,' I told him, before the make-or-break game with Juventus. I was right. We lost two-nil.

But analogies have to break down somewhere. The mind weaves its web across the world, seeking out similarities, tying together like and like, insisting, grasping, imagining it has understood. But if analogy didn't end, if two things were alike in every way, then they would cancel each other out, and so cease to exist in a sense. We would only have that mental web and nothing left to catch in it. 'It's insulting,' my wife said one evening, 'the way you keep comparing Marina and Giorgio's troubles to the football season. It's ridiculous,' she complained. And she was right. For in the end I didn't really give a damn if Verona went into Serie B. Or Serie C for that matter. In the end I couldn't give a tinker's curse whether they beat Milan or lost to lowly Reggiana ten-nil. Whether they won the World Cup all on their own or went bankrupt and closed down for ever. It didn't matter to me at all. Whereas it would be a major cataclysm in four people's lives – no way round that – if Giorgio chose to leave his family for good. However exciting it is when the terraces fill and the flags wave and the players chase brilliant colours over dazzling green, the stadium is only a small place in the large city, the larger universe of the mind, a small theatre where wonderfully infantile pleasures can be endlessly re-enacted. Whereas a sitting room is huge. A child gigantic. And the bedroom a cosmos. 'I only do that,' I told her, 'because it's the only way you'll let me talk about football.'

So at the darkest moment of the season – mathematical relegation – Giorgio went home. Not beaten at all, but saying, This is what I want, my marriage, this is what I choose. Triumphant, in fact. As if emerging from a shadow. From a spell. The enchantment of Raffaella. Or of my analogy. 'How could I imagine I didn't love my wife?' he said. 'How could I think of living away from the kids?' And as we sat among a dwindling and despondent crowd to see the last rites played out against Parma, the curtain come down on our flirtation with Serie A, he said, 'Well, thank God *I'm* not going down.' And he said: 'Nothing easier than firing the poor girl when it came to it.' 'Bit of a loss of entertainment for me,' I complained. Later that evening, when my own wife finally got off the phone with a very chatty Marina, I said gloomily, 'And they've renewed Cagni's contract too. Can you believe it? Does nothing ever end?' 'Let's drink to marriage,' she said. Then she laughed, 'For one more season.' The following week I went down to the stadium with Michele and ordered next year's tickets.